THE BRIDGESTONE VEGETARIAN GUIDE TO IRELAND

GW00375239

THE BRIDGESTONE

VEGETARIAN

GUIDE TO IRELAND

JOHN McKENNA - SALLY McKENNA

ESTRAGON PRESS

FIRST PUBLISHED IN 2002

BY ESTRAGON PRESS

DURRUS

COUNTY CORK

© ESTRAGON PRESS

TEXT © JOHN & SALLY McKENNA

THE MORAL RIGHT OF THE AUTHORS

HAS BEEN ASSERTED

ISBN 1 874076 36 7

PRINTED IN SPAIN BY GRAPHYCEMS

• The Bridgestone Vegetarian Guide to Ireland is arranged **ALPHABETICALLY, BY COUNTY** so it begins with County Carlow, which is followed by County Cavan, and so on.

• Within the counties, the entries are designated as where to eat, where to stay, and where to shop, with further categories describing specialist producers.

• Entries in Northern Ireland are described at the end of the book.

• The contents of the Bridgestone Vegetarian Guide are exclusively the result of the editors' deliberations. All meals and accommodation were paid for and any offers of discounts or gifts were refused.

• Many of the places featured in this book are only open during the summer season, which means that they can be closed for any given length of time between October and March. Many others change their opening times during the winter season.

• **PRICES:** Dinner prices are calculated for an average three course menu, without wine. In this book we have elected to give price ranges, using the euro symbol as follows: under €10 = €; €10-€25 = €€; €25-€35 = €€€; over €35 = €€€€; over €45 = €€€€€. Accommodation rates are approximately calculated thus: Modest = €; mid-priced = €€; luxury = €€€. All prices and details are correct at the time of going to press, but please use these figures merely as a guide.

• Finally, we greatly appreciate receiving reports, suggestions and criticisms from readers, and would like to thank those who have written in the past, whose opinions are of enormous assistance to us when considering which establishments finally make it into this book.

CONTENTS

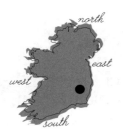

County
Carlow

north

east

west

south

EATING

● **Lennon's Café Bar** Sinéad Byrne's
bright, busy bar puts out some of the
smartest, most delicious bar food
you can eat: spinach, roast pepper
and tomato roulade; roasted peppers
with Wilton tomatoes topped with
goat's cheese; roasted vegetable wrap
with pesto; couscous with summer vegetables;
butterbean casserole with cider; courgette, aubergine
and cheese bake. Great staff, great value, great
place. (121 Tullow St, Carlow, Tel: (0503) 31575. Open
Lunch, €€)

STAYING

● **Kilgraney Country House** Martin
and Bryan's gorgeous country house
now boasts a series of terrific self-
catering apartments carved out of
the old courtyard at the rere of the
house. Kilgraney is one of the cult
addresses, thanks to superb cooking
from Bryan, and those who want an escape from the
city should really explore the stunning quietude of this
lovely valley.
(Bagenalstown, Tel: (0503) 75283 Fax: 75595
kilgrany@indigo.ie www.kilgraneyhouse.com Open:
February-November, Dinner €€€, Rooms €€)

SHOPPING

● The Carlow Craft Brewery

Whilst the magisterial O'Hara's stout has been the benchmark brew of the inspiring Carlow Brewing Co, the red ale Molings and the thirst-quenching wheat beer Curim are two superb brews in their own right. For our money these are some of the best drinks you can find in Ireland, and when you get a taste of that O'Hara's, with its roasty, toasty, malty sharpness, it's a moment of pure bliss. (The Goods Store, Station Rd, Carlow Tel: (0503) 34356, Fax: 40038, ccb@iol.ie)

County
Cavan

EATING & STAYING

● **MacNean Bistro** Neven Maguire is the finest young chef in Ireland, and one of the most thoughtful, as evidenced by his special vegetarian menu which is one of the MacNean's best sellers. Warm potato pancake with sautéed mushrooms and crème fraîche; crispy goat's cheese with basil oil; grilled polenta with avocado spring roll and chilli jam; egg noodles with fennel, peas and truffle oil; warm salad of grilled vegetables with aged balsamic, superlative salads from Eden Herbs and, then, the very best desserts you can find in Ireland. Make sure to book a room and stay overnight and make the most of the MacNean. (MacNean Bistro, Blacklion, Tel: (072) 53022 Fax: (072) 53404. Open: 6pm-9pm Tue-Sun, 1pm & 3.15pm Sun, Meals €€€, Rooms €€)

SHOPPING

● **Back To Nature** Look out for lots of fine
vegetarian and wholefoods in Christine McGuinness's
Cavan health store. (Main Street, Cavan, Tel: (049)
961019)

● **Boilie** Small, soft orbs of goat's milk and cow's
milk cheeses preserved in oil and available
everywhere. One of the very best artisan foods to
enter the mainstream. (Ryefield Farm, Bailieboro, Tel:
(042) 966 6848, info@ryefield.com, ryefield.com)

● **Corleggy** Silke Cropp's Corleggy is one of the
most delicious and redoubtable of Irish farmhouse
cheeses, mottled, khaki-brown rinded small truckles
of fudgey-sweet goat's milk, to be hunted down in
markets here and there, where you will find it sold
with panache and style by the cheesemaker.
(Belturbet, Tel: (049) 952 2930, corleggy@eircom.net)

● **Planet Earth** Good, local healthfood store, run
by Diane Crook. (Lower Main Street, Bailieboro)

 County
Clare

EATING

● **Barrtrá** This cute little him 'n' her restaurant
overlooking Liscannor Bay has been a happy home
from home for holidaymakers and locals for more
than a decade. The very personal service means the
small selection of vegetarian dishes are always
carefully delivered: feta and wild mushroom filo
parcel; spinach and St Tola goat's cheese pancake.
(Barrtrá, Lahinch, Tel: (065) 708 1280 Open: 5pm-
10pm Tue-Sun (closed Nov-Jan, open 7 days high
season), Dinner €€€)

● **Cherry Tree Restaurant** A hip, hot, waterside spot with dynamic vegetarian cooking? It sounds too good to be true, doesn't it, but Harry McGeough and his young team have made the gorgeous Cherry Tree the toast of the region for some scintillating food – fritters of organic asparagus with aioli and roast piquillo peppers with a black olive vinaigrette; cappuccino of organic spinach soup; crostini of Bluebell Falls goat's cheese with ratatouille; Malaysian laksa with stir-fried bak choi, shiitake and Thai red curry sauce. McGeough and his team cook this food with real accomplishment, understanding everything about the ingredients from source all the way to ultimate satisfaction. An unmissable address, and don't imagine you have to go messing about on boats to head to Killaloe. (Lakeside, Ballina, Killaloe, Tel: (061) 375688, Fax: (061) 375689, Open: 6pm-10pm Tue-Sat, 6pm-10pm Sun & Bank hols, Dinner €€€€)

● **Doolin Café** This is where all the musicians and music lover's hang out during Doolin's endless musical summer, and it's a nicely laid-back chill-out spot. (Doolin, Tel: (065) 707 4795, Open lunch & dinner, Lunch €, Dinner €€)

● **Flappers** Patricia Cahill has a lovely touch as a cook, so whilst her food can read as simple signature dishes – garlic mushrooms in puff pastry; vegetable lasagne with pesto bread; aubergine gateau; goat's cheese pithiviers with tapenade – the sheer goodness of the ingredients and the quality and élan of the cooking makes for super food. The room itself is small and sweet, the staff are motherly and attentive. (Main Street, Tulla, Tel: (065) 6835711, Open: Noon-3pm Mon-Sat, 7pm-9.45pm Tue-Sat (winter open noon-3pm Mon-Sat, 7pm-9.30pm Thur-Sat), Dinner €€€)

● **Henry's Deli** Ice cream and coffees are why the locals head to Henry's at the car park. It's a nice room with some nice food and Henry's hangdog style is always a hoot.
(Riverside House, Abbey St Car Park, Ennis, Tel: (065) 682 2848. Open Lunch, €)

● **The Mermaid** Neville and Kathi's little restaurant is a true humdinger that you should not miss. The cooking has real chutzpah: polenta gateau with roast vegetables; Kilshanny cumin cheese with carrot and mushroom bake; Thai vegetable curry with spinach and almonds.
Lovely beers, mighty atmosphere, great craic. (The Mermaid, Liscannor Village, Liscannor, Tel: (065) 7081076 themermaid@ireland.com Open: 6pm-11pm Mon-Sun. Closed Nov-Mar) Dinner €€€)

● **The Tea Junction Café** This is a popular place right smack at the junction in Ballyvaughan, especially for breakfast and some nicely considered, real lunch foods in the form of salads, wraps, rolls and sandwiches.
(The Tea Junction Café, Ballyvaughan, Tel: (065) 707 7289, Open daily, Meals €)

● **The Whitethorn** John and Sarah McDonnell's swish and smart restaurant and craft centre belies its self-service style with some really delicious food: char-grilled aubergine with spinach, walnuts and blue cheese with tomato relish; Mediterranean tartlets of pesto, pine nuts, Parmesan and olives; Parmesan filo bake with sweet peppers, onions and almonds. Terrific views across the bay, so pull up a chair, slap on those shades and order up a glass of Chardonnay.
(Ballyvaughan, Tel: (065) 707 7023, Open daily, Meals €€)

STAYING

● **Fergus View** The rooms are simple, but Mary Kelleher's welcome is true and her cooking is very, very tasty, the sort of food you dream about sitting down to after a soaking hike through the Burren: mushroom and tarragon crepe; local Poulcoin goat's cheese in a potato gratin; scrummy garden vegetables, and there are great breakfasts to get you out the door in the morning and set off on that soaking hike once more. (Fergus View, Kilnaboy, Corofin, Tel: (065) 683 7606, Fax: 683 7192 deckell@indigo.ie Open: Easter-mid Oct, Rooms €)

BREWS AND TIPPLES

Biddy Early Brew Pub
Black Biddy, Red Biddy and White Biddy are the trio of beers which re-started the brewing revolution in Ireland, and while you can now find them further afield than Inagh – where they are sold in the Biddy Early pub where they are also made – there is nothing quite like a pint or a bottle of these fine brews enjoyed in their County Clare birthplace. (Inagh, Tel: (065) 683 6742, info@beb.ie, beb.ie)

Patrick Egan's Pub
Patrick Egan's pub is a legend in its own lifetime, a place for great pints and great craic, but also a repository of extraordinary wines, thanks to the boss's predilection for great clarets. The range of superstar wines on sale here is gobsmacking. Look out also for the brilliant Spanish wines of Rafael Alvarez which Patrick sells. (Liscannor, Tel: (065) 7081784/7081430)

SHOPPING

● **Bluebell Falls Goat's Cheese** Paul Keane's fresh goat's milk cheeses manage to pack a mighty flavour punch, despite being sold when still in their infancy. We don't know how he manages to extract such a ton of flavour but we're glad he does. Don't miss the Bluebell Falls in local shops and restaurants. (Ballynacally, Tel: (065) 683 8024)

● **Burren Gold** Buying Ben Johnson's fine, sweet cheeses is a must-do when making a pilgrimage to the splendid Aillwee Caves. You can scarcely find this cheese beyond the Clare borders, so it's another vital destination, and there are good preserves and chocolates to be enjoyed in the shop. (Ballyvaughan, Tel: (065) 7077036, Fax: 7077107, aillweecave.ie)

● **Clare Jam Company** The reputation of Vera and David Muir's jams is spreading, and deservedly so, for these are well-made, fruit driven jams of fine quality. (Lough North, Doolin, Tel: (065) 707 4778, Fax: 707 4871 clarejam@eircom.net)

● **Cratloe Hills Sheep's Cheese** Look out for the small, golden orbs (snitchs, perhaps, Harry Potter fans?) of Cratloe, for these dense little rounds of sheep's milk cheese are superbly made, and are a great boon for the cook, for when grated they offer a true and delicious alternative to Parmesan. The snitchs of Cratloe are widely available. (Cratloe, Tel: (061) 357185)

● **Kilshanny Cheese** Kilshanny is almost a staple of County Clare cuisine, used by the best chefs, and sold at many of the local markets by Amanda Nibbering and Dick de Valk. Flavoured with various herbs and spices, these are quixotic and beautifully made Gouda-style cheeses. (Lahinch, Tel: (065) 707 1228)

● **Poulcoin Cheese** Anneliese Bartelink's cheese is one of the most difficult to find in Ireland, and one of the most rewarding to discover when you do get your hands on it. The small orbs of Gouda-style cheese simply burst with the zesty zing of pure milk. Your mission in County Clare – and we know you will accept it – must include hunting down Poulcoin cheese. (Telephone number withheld, and the cheese is not available from the farm. Hunt it down in local shops and B&Bs)

● **St Tola** John McDonnell's fine, mild goat's milk cheeses are made to organic standards, and whether you buy the small, fresh crottins or the longer, more mature rolls, you buy into beautiful, unalloyed freshness and sweetness. Available to buy also from the farm. (Inagh, Tel: (065) 683 6633, saint.tola@iol.ie)

GREAT VILLAGE STORES

Ennis Gourmet Store Anne Leyden's excellent shop – and its sister Café des Gourmets, just across the street – are great spots not just for interesting lunches and snacks, but also for sourcing the best foods of the county. Don't miss their exceptionally fine hampers for special occasions. (1 Barrack St, Ennis, Tel: (065) 684 3314, gourmetstore@eircom.net)

Open Sesame A vital address for organic vegetables, for details of box delivery systems, and also for essential wholefoods, all of which make their way to this snazzy, bright, fun shop. (29 Parnell St, Ennis, Tel: (065) 682 1480)

Unglert's Bakery A delightful, squishy-bun sort of local bakery, with moreish sweet things and utterly charming, modest service. (Ennistymon, Tel: (065) 707 1217)

The Village Stores Sheila McGannon's smart Spar shop has all the good local foods. (Ballyvaughan, Tel: (065) 707 7181 villagestores@eircom.net)

10 RESTAURANTS
WITH GREAT SERVICE

1
AVOCA
DUBLIN

2
CAFÉ PARADISO
CORK CITY

3
DISH
DUBLIN

4
L'ECRIVAIN
DUBLIN

5
JUICE
DUBLIN

6
KILARNEY PARK
KILLARNEY

7
LEFT BANK BISTRO
ATHLONE

8
LA MARINE
ROSSLARE

9
NIMMOS
GALWAY

10
SHEEN FALLS
KENMARE

County
Cork

CORK CITY
– WHERE FIRST?

● ● ● ● ● ● ● ● ● ● ● ● ● ● ● ● ●

● **Café Paradiso** Denis Cotter is the finest vegetarian cook in these islands, and with Bridget Healy he runs the finest vegetarian restaurant in these islands. Café Paradiso is the magical confection of a truly original cook, a man who not only puts his ideas into delicious practice every day of the week, but whose theories on the subject of vegetarian cooking, as evidenced by his outstanding book "The Café Paradiso Cookbook", have led to what we believe is the finest cookery book ever written by any chef anywhere. If you can't live without the book, you can't live without the restaurant. Democratic, fun, distinct, there is no other room like it. Potato and watercress gnocchi in a roasted tomato cream is both light and yet gutsy, and when that watercress appears again in a risotto with avocado and a stew of cannelloni beans it serves a wholly different role, this time drawing out the flavours of the avocado. This is what makes Denis Cotter's work so special, the way in which ingredients are played with like so many themes in a piece of music, juxtaposed, counterpointed, often just plain improvised. Great wines, great sounds, great service, and one of the greatest Irish restaurants of all time. (16 Lancaster Quay, Cork, Tel: (021) 427 7939, Fax: 427 4973 cafeparadiso.ie Open: 12.30pm-3pm, 6.30pm-10.30pm Tue-Sat. Lunch €€, Dinner €€€€)

● **Natural Foods** The Natural is one
of the key wholefood shops in the city,
invaluable for vital foods and
vegetables, and for excellent breads.
NF has been around for a long time,
but it's a place which is forever young.
(26 Paul St, Tel: (021) 427 7244)

● **The Quay Co-Op** The shop at the Quay is one of
the very best, always offering some
intriguing new things, always
expanding its range. Upstairs in the
long-established restaurant,
however, the atmosphere is less
progressive. This is very much old-style
vegetarian cooking, where staples are used to imitate
meat, rather than finding a taste expression of their
own. Some new energy is needed to bring the QC-O
into the new age. (24 Sullivan's Quay, Tel: (021) 431
7660)

CORK CITY
– WHERE NEXT?

● **Crawford Gallery Café**
This beautifully serene space is a city outpost of the
Ballymaloe empire, and wisely practices the
Ballymaloe philosophy. The Crawford is quite one of
the nicest places to take lunch, as well as morning
coffee or afternoon tea. (Crawford Gallery, Emmet
Place, Tel: (021) 427 4415, Open Lunch €€)

● **Idaho.café** A darling little corner space with
darling cooking, right from fine breakfasts – Belgian
waffles with maple syrup; hot porridge; good scones
and jam – through to lunch – tartlet of minty peas with
organic goat's cheese; grilled sweet pepper bapini –
and some seriously delicious sweet things. Brilliant.
(19 Caroline Street, Cork, Tel: (021) 4276 376)

● **The Ivory Tower** Seamus O'Connell is a cook like no other. Mercurial as all get out, his focus is entirely on the immediacy of the cooking act, so virtually everything in the IT is cooked in the instant, improvised on the spot. It can be an experience exhilarating beyond belief, and for some who expect the formalities of a standard restaurant, it can be frustrating beyond belief. If you get it, there is nowhere else like the 'Tower. (The Exchange Buildings, 35 Princes Street, Tel: (021) 427 4665, Open Dinner €€€)

● **Jacob's on the Mall** Jacob's has always offered thoughtful and polished vegetarian cooking: spicy tomato and lentil soup; goat's cheese with grilled vegetables and caramelised onion in filo; spaghetti with pesto, pine nuts and smoked sundried tomatoes; summer couscous salad with marinated vegetables; artichoke and mushroom potato cake with lentil vinaigrette. (30a South Mall, Tel: (021) 425 1530, Fax 425 1531 kingsley@tinet.ie Open: 12.30pm-2.30pm, 6.30pm-10pm Mon-Sat, Lunch €€, Dinner €€€)

● **Jacques** Jacques always seems to have just what you feel like eating: angel hair with forest mushrooms, cashews and garlic cream; their excellent vegetable plate with portobellos stuffed with cheese and nuts. And do take their advice and kick things off with a half bottle of manzanilla and some nuts and olives. Mighty. (Phoenix Street, Cork, Tel: (021) 4277387, Fax: 4270634 Open: Noon-3pm Mon-Fri, 6pm-10pm Tue-Sat, Lunch €€, Dinner €€€)

● **Wildways** Good coffees and food-to-go are the thing in this stylish and organically-focused café.(21 Princes St, Cork, www.wildways.net, open daily, Lunch €)

10 GREAT STALLS IN
THE ENGLISH MARKET

1
ALTERNATIVE BREAD CO
CHOICE, CLEVER BAKING

2
ARBUTUS BREADS
BEST BREAD MADE IN IRELAND

3
MR BELL'S
MULTI-CULTURAL CULINARY DESIRES

4
BUBBLE BROTHERS
GREAT WINES AND CHAMPAGNES

5
CAFÉ CENTRAL
A DEMON CUP OF COFFEE

6
THE FARM GATE
A BOISTEROUS TREAT

7
THE GARDEN
FRESHLY PICKED, ORGANIC

8
IAGO
SUPERB PASTAS AND SAUCES

9
THE ORGANIC SHOP
EXTENSIVE & EXHAUSTIVE

10
REAL OLIVE CO
GREAT OLIVES, GREAT FOODS

THE OTHER MARKET

● **The Cornmarket Market** In addition to the
English Market in the centre of the city
(see left) a variety of organic
producers set up stalls in front of the
Bodega on Cornmarket Street on
Saturday mornings. Organic growers
such as Caroline Robinson have built up
a devoted following for their thunderously good
produce, so you need to be here early in the morning
or everything will be snapped up. (Open Saturday
mornings)

STAYING

● **Seven North Mall** A serene and stylish
townhouse which is many people's first choice in the
southern capital. (7 North Mall, Cork, Tel: (021) 439
7191, Fax: 430 0811 sevennorthmall@eircom.net
Open: All year, except Christmas, Rooms €€)

ANYTHING ELSE?

Maher's Coffee
A tiny shop with a big reputation, Maher's roasts some
seriously fine coffees. A bag of the Italian roast for us,
please. (25 Oliver Plunkett St, Tel: (021) 427 0008)

Eve's Chocolates
Eve St. Leger's chocolates are the stuff of
legend. Once you have the fantastic (and
utterly unique) Corkies, you can no
longer live without them, and once your
kids have tried the 1-metre long Metre
of Chocolate, they will be just as
addicted as you. An unmissable and
magical little choccie shop. (College Commercial Park,
Magazine Rd, Tel: (021) 434 7781)

COUNTY CORK
– LET'S GO EAST

● ● ● ● ● ● ● ● ● ● ● ● ● ● ● ● ● ●

EATING

● **The Cross of Cloyne** The vegetarian choices in Colm Falvey's swish restaurant are small – he likes to work with the excellent local Ardsallagh goat's cheese, and makes some very assured pasta dishes and risottos – but the quality of ingredients and the flair of the cooking are attraction enough to bring you to this room. (Cloyne, nr Midleton, Tel: (021) 465 2401 Fax: 465 2401, Open: 6pm-9.30pm Wed-Sun (from 4pm Sun), Dinner €€€)

● **Ballymaloe House** The legendary Ballymaloe has always offered creative and elegantly composed vegetarian dishes as part of the dinner choices, with the dishes reflecting the pre-eminence this famous house places on immaculate ingredients. To eat the garden asparagus, the garden salad leaves, the seasonal vegetables they serve is to be confronted with tastes of purest deliciousness, whilst the use of local cheeses such as Knockalara sheep's cheese with a Provençale stew of beans is a delight. (Shanagarry, Co Cork, Tel: (021) 465 2531, Fax: 465 2029 res@ballymaloe.ie www.ballymaloe.com Open: 1pm-1.30pm, 7pm-9.30pm Mon-Sun, Dinner €€€€€. Rooms €€€)

● **The Farmgate** Marog O'Brien's fine café, restaurant and shop is one of the east Cork legends. You will also find their breads for sale at the Saturday Midleton market. (Midleton, Tel: (021) 463 2771)

COUNTY CORK MARKETS

Bantry
The first Friday of each month is fair day in Bantry, and it brings to the town a brilliant collection of artisans and producers.

Carrigaline
Carrigaline Friday morning Country Market is one of the best country markets in Ireland, and a great local institution. (Kilnagleary, Carrigaline, Tel: (021) 437 2864)

Castletownbere
The first Thursday Market has local artisans and other marketeers here on the first Thursday of each month.

Clonakilty
The Clonakilty Market takes place each Thursday. Don't miss the market in town, and look out for cheeses from Fiona Burke, splendid foods and breads from Clodagh McKenna, organic foods from Mark O'Mahoney amongst other choice artisan foods.

Midleton
The Midleton Saturday Market is unmissable, with loads of seasonal delights and charming stallholders. (SuperValu carpark, Saturday mornings)

Skibbereen
The Saturday Morning Market is a great local market: look out in particular for Jean Perry's beautiful vegetables and flowers, and Fingal Ferguson's Big Smokie cheese.

STAYING

● **Glenally House** Another triumphant piece of modernist design in east Cork, Fred and Herta Rigney's peach of a house is a dream destination for design heads. (Copperally, Youghal, Co Cork, Tel: (024) 91623 enquiries@glenally.com www.glenally.com Open: All year. Reservations only Nov-Feb, Rooms €€)

● **Rathcoursey House** Beth Hallinan's glorious house is a showcase of stupendous style choices. Stay here and, as well as having a ball, you will get a zillion design ideas. (Ballinacurra, Midleton, East Cork Tel: (021) 461 3418, beth@rathcoursey.com www.rathcoursey.com Open: all year, Rooms €€€)

SHOPPING

● **Ballymaloe Shop** An utter delight, every object chosen with extreme care. (Ballymaloe House, Shanagarry, Tel: (021) 465 2032)

● **Macroom Oatmeal** Legendary oatmeal, cooked, for example, as part of the breakfast in Zingerman's legendary deli in Ann Arbor, USA. (Macroom, Tel: (026) 41800)

● **O'Callaghan's Deli** The quiches and Mediterranean sandwiches are great, as are the desserts. (Lower Cork St, Mitchelstown, Tel: (025) 24657)

● **Well & Good** Superb wholefood shop, run by Jill Bell, one of the pioneers of the Free Choice Consumer Group. Great for local veg, and rarities such as the sublime Traas apple juice. (Broderick St, Midleton, Tel: (021) 463 3499)

10 GREAT
WEST CORK CHEESES

1

ARDRAHAN
PACKS IN FLAVOUR

2

CARRAIG
WORTH HUNTING DOWN

3

CARRIGALINE
AWARD-WINNING TALENT

4

COOLEA
BLOW-ME AWAY FUDGEYNESS

5

DURRUS
A FOOD LOVER'S TREASURE

6

GABRIEL & DESMOND
PIQUANT AND PINEAPPLEY

7

GUBBEEN
UTTERLY DISTINCTIVE

8

MILLEENS
A LEGENDARY CHEESE

9

BIG SMOKIE
GUBBEEN'S MARKET CHEESE

10

ROUND TOWER
A MID WEST CORK SECRET

COUNTY CORK
– LET'S GO WEST

● ● ● ● ● ● ● ● ● ● ● ● ● ● ● ● ● ● ●

EATING

● **Adèle's Bakery** One of the quintessential west Cork addresses, this pretty café, tea rooms and accommodation (four simple rooms at the top of the stairs) is a delight, and just don't leave without a lemon cake. (Main St, Schull, Tel: (028) 28459, adelesrestaurant.com)

● **Fionnuala's Little Italian Restaurant**
Simple, accessible and quite delicious cooking is the order of the day from Fionnuala and her dedicated team. Charming. (30 Ashe St, Clonakilty, Tel: (023) 34355, Open Dinner €€)

● **Kalbo's** Kalbo's is the destination address in Skibb for friendly, flavourful cooking, achieved with flair and panache and no little style: a key address. And, directly across the street, their deli is also spot on, and a great source of interesting breads and other interesting foods. (North St, Skibbereen, Tel: (028) 21515, Open Lunch, €€ and Dinner €€€€)

● **Longueville House** William O'Callaghan is one of Ireland's most incisively creative chefs, and the brio he shows with his cooking is ex-hilarating: avocado mousse with a salad of garden leeks; local Ardrahan cheese in a pastry with hazelnut sauce is a delight. Fabulous desserts, great service, sublime. (Mallow, Tel: (022) 47156, Fax: 47459 info@longuevillehouse.ie www.longuevillehouse.ie Open: 7pm-9pm Mon-Sun, Dinner €€€€€, Rooms €€€)

STAYING

● **Assolas Country House** This pretty and modestly grand house is home to Joe and Hazel Bourke, and Mrs Bourke's cooking is, for us, some of the finest to be enjoyed in Ireland. The sheer quality of garden vegetables makes a dish such as spinach tart with caramelised onions and Cashel Blue cheese unforgettable, whilst even simple things such as tomato tarte tatin are glorious. (Kanturk, Tel: (029) 50015, Fax: 60795, assolas@eircom.net, assolas.com, Rooms €€€)

● **Blindgate House** A style lover's dream is what Maeve Coakley has concocted in Blindgate, the cult address in Kinsale. Beautiful rooms, super breakfasts, all done with enviable precision. (Blindgate, Kinsale, Tel: (021) 477 7858, Fax: 477 7868 info@blindgatehouse.com blindgatehouse.com Open Mar-Oct, Rooms €€)

● **Fortview House** Violet Connell's West Cork B&B is one of the best-loved bed and breakfasts in the entire country, and a great base for exploring all the peninsulas. (Gurtyowen, Toormore, Goleen, West Cork, Tel & Fax: (028) 35324 fortviewhousegoleen@eircom.net www.westcorkweb.ie/fortview Open 1 March-1 Nov Rooms €€)

● **Grove House** The best house in beautiful Schull looks out over the sea, and has great breakfasts and great hospitality. Colla Road, Schull, West Cork, Tel: (028) 28067, Fax: 28069 billyoshea@yahoo.com www.cork-guide.ie/schull/grove/welcome.html Open Mar-Sep (Nov-Feb by arrangement), Rooms €€)

SHOPPING

● **Fruit Hill Farm** Manfred Wandel sells some of the best gardening tools and gardening supplies you can buy, and look out for the organic produce of Fruit Hill Farm, all of which is of superb quality. (Bantry, Tel: (027) 50710)

● **Karwig Wines** It's tricky to find Joe Karwig's excellent wine shop, but one visit will leave you hooked. Like all the best merchants, the list is curious, personal, intriguing, and service is great. (Kilnagleary, Carrigaline, Tel: (021) 437 2864)

● **Mrs Collins Ice Cream** Mrs Collins' is one of the best ice creams made in Ireland, and hunting it down in shops in West Cork should be on your agenda. Look out especially for the winter berry ice cream. (Castlewhite, Waterfall, Tel: (021) 434 2050)

● **West Cork Herb Farm** Look out for Rosarie and Kevin's unique range of herb-infused condiments and jellies in good shops and supermarkets. The green peppercorn mustard is a don't-miss! (Church Cross, Skibbereen, Tel: (028) 38428)

GREAT COUNTRY SHOPS

The Courtyard
A beautiful bar, lovely tea rooms and an excellent deli and wine shop. A sandwich and a pint in front of the fire in the bar on a chill winter day in the Courtyard is pure bliss. (Main St, Schull, Tel: (028) 28390)

Field's
The best small supermarket in the country is magnificent right across the board, with every manner of specialist food and an inimitable atmosphere. (26 Main St, Skibbereen, Tel: (028) 21400)

Manning's Food Emporium
A venerable West Cork institution, renowned for a great cheese counter. (Ballylickey, Tel: (027) 50456)

The Quay Food Co
Excellent deli which is a don't-miss in pretty Kinsale, especially if you want to assemble a picnic of choice deli foods. (Market Quay, Kinsale, Tel: (021) 477 4000, quayfood@hotmail.com)

GREAT WHOLEFOOD SHOPS

Bantry Wholefoods
Simon's excellent shop has lots of rare West Cork specialities along with essential wholefoods. (Bridewell Lane, Bantry Tel: (027) 52611)

Hudson's Wholefoods
Some of the most imaginative wraps and sandwiches you can find are served here in the café of Gill Hudson's excellent wholefood shop, and you can take them away for a picnic also. (Main St, Ballydehob, Tel: (028) 37211)

Organico
Don't miss the breads, pizza slices, samosas and sushi you will find here, in addition to a zillion other fine foods in one of the key West Cork shops. (Glengarriff Rd, Bantry, Tel: (027) 51391)

Organic Oasis
Caroline Weese's pretty and intimate shop has all the wholefoods you need plus local vegetables and other West Cork specialities. (Main St, Schull, Tel: (028) 28533)

Yin Yang
A fine wholefood shop with excellent service. (Market St, Skibbereen, Tel: (028) 22537)

10 GREAT
MARKETS

1
BROOK LODGE INN MARKET
CO WICKLOW

2
CARRIGALINE MARKET
CO CORK

3
COW'S LANE MARKET
DUBLIN

4
THE GALWAY MARKET
CO GALWAY

5
KILTERNAN COUNTRY MARKET
CO WICKLOW

6
MIDLETON FARMERS' MARKET
CO CORK

7
NAAS COUNTRY MARKET
CO KILDARE

8
ST GEORGE'S MARKET
BELFAST

9
TEMPLE BAR MARKET
DUBLIN

10
WESTPORT MARKET
CO MAYO

County **Donegal**

EATING

● **Castlemurray House** Newly taken over by Marguerite Howley, Castlemurray is destined for greatness once again. One of the key restaurants with rooms, with awesome views. (St John's Point, Dunkineely, Tel: (073) 37022, Fax: 37330, castlemurray@eircom.net, Open Dinner €€€, Rates €€)

● **McGrory's** Neil McGrory's bar and restaurant is a cult local address with very thoughtful and helpful staff, nice cooking, and great music sessions. (Culdaff, Tel: (077) 79104, Open Lunch € and Dinner €€)

STAYING

● **The Green Gate** Arcadian simplicity won't appeal to all, but if you cherish a rustic retreat, The Green Gate is unique. (Ardvally, Ardara, Tel: (075) 41546 Open: All year, Rates €)

● **The Mill Restaurant & Accommodation** A beautiful location in farthest Donegal is as much of a treat as the fine cooking such as leek and wild mushroom stroganoff with sage and ginger. A lovely escape, for sure. (Figart, Dunfanaghy, Letterkenny, Tel/Fax: (074) 36985 themillrestaurant@oceanfree.net www.themillrestaurant.com Open: 7pm-9pm, 12.30pm-2pm Sun, Lunch €€, Dinner €€€, Rooms €€)

SHOPPING

● **Thomas Becht** Thomas Becht is a pioneer grower, silviculturist and cheesemaker, and he has a fine box delivery system to make sure you get superb vegetables. (Dorian, Glenties, Tel: (075) 51286)

● **De Vine Wines** Lots of cleverly sourced wines, including some from the brilliant Searson's of Dublin, characterise this fine wine shop. (Pearse Rd, Letterkenny, Tel: (074) 71730)

● **Dibbles** Roisin Jenkin's Dibbles relishes and salad dressings are benchmark foods (Port na Blagh, Tel: (074) 36655, roisin@dibbles.ie, dibbles.ie)

● **Filligans** Philip and Sarah Moss make the most delectable relishes and jams, and also magically delicious cakes. (Glenties, Tel: (075) 51628, moss@gofree.indigo.ie)

● **North West Organic Producers' Group** A key contact for sourcing the foods of this cross-border group of organic producers. (Copley, Muff, Tel: (077) 84107 nwopg@eircom.net)

FOOD FOR HEALTH

Simple Simon is one of the very best wholefood shops, run with genial authority by Andrew Cape and home to many of the best foods in the north west, as well as many interesting foods cooked on the premises. Two other essential destinations for whole and health foods are Letterkenny's Natural Way, run by David Foley and Paul Brogan's Food For Thought in Buncrana. (Simple Simon, Anderson's Yard, The Diamond, Donegal Tel: (073) 22687) (The Natural Way, Unit 3, Letterkenny Shopping Centre, Letterkenny Tel: (074) 25738) (Food For Thought, Lower Main St, Buncrana Tel: (077) 63550)

 County **Dublin**

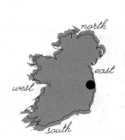

COOL, CASUAL EATING

NORTHSIDE
● ● ● ● ● ● ● ● ● ● ● ●

● **Aqua** It's a long trek out to Howth, but Aqua's combination of a stylish room with great views and some interesting cooking – tortellini gorgonzola with black olives; grilled asparagus with roasted peppers; buffalo mozzarella with baby greens – makes the jaunt worthwhile. (1 West Pier, Howth, Co Dublin, Tel: (01) 832 0690, Fax: 832 0687, dine@aqua.ie www.aqua.ie, Open Lunch €€ and Dinner €€€)

● **Bond** Karl Purdy and his team run a great room with perhaps the city's finest choice of wines, but the cooking is no slouch either: the stack of grilled aubergine and ratatouille with feta and a charred tomato and balsamic reduction is spot on; roasted Portobello mushrooms with pesto and wilted Swiss chard is just right, and the salads and pastas are very imaginative. (5 Beresford Place, Dublin 1 Tel: (01) 855 9244, Open Lunch €€ and Dinner €€€€)

● **Expresso Café** Part of the huge IFSC complex, Expresso has a southside sister in Ballsbridge which serves food just as hip to the trip as this stylish room. (The IFSC, Dublin 1, Tel: (01) 672 1812, Open Lunch €)

10 GREAT PLACES
FOR THE WEEKEND

1

BOLTOWN HOUSE
CO MEATH

2

BROOK LODGE INN
CO WICKLOW

3

GHAN HOUSE
CO LOUTH

4

HANORA'S COTTAGE
CO WATERFORD

5

KILGRANEY HOUSE
CO CARLOW

6

RICHMOND HOUSE
CO WATERFORD

7

SALVILLE HOUSE
CO WEXFORD

8

TEMPLE SPA
CO WESTMEATH

9

WINEPORT LODGE
CO WESTMEATH

10

ZUNI
CO KILKENNY

● **Il Fornaio** The pizzas in this cult little address in Raheny are the object of your desire, with lots of good choices amidst the strangest names for pizzas ever devised. (55 Kilbarrack Rd, Raheny, D5, Tel: 1890 482542, Open daily, €)

● **Halo** The vegetarian choices in this ultra-smart city hotel are always provocative and considered – butternut squash and Parmesan soup with celeriac; baked courgettes with pepper stew and a Parmesan cream – but to be honest, the things not to miss are the ab fab desserts, which are perhaps the best in the city. (Morrison Hotel Ormond Quay, Dublin 1, Tel: (01) 887 2421, Fax: 878 3185 info@morrisonhotel.ie www.morrisonhotel.ie Open all year: Lunch €€€, Dinner €€€€, Rooms €€€)

● **Itsabagel** The Kemp sisters have another branch of 'bagel out in Dun Laoghaire, whilst their original northside emporium packs in the happy punters day after day for cracking bagels, good drinks and good fun. (Epicurean Mall, D1, Tel: (01) 874 0486, itsabagel.com, Open daily, Lunch €)

● **Mero Mero Café** Gus and Theresa Hernandez understand Mexican food like no one else in Ireland, and Mero Mero is a don't-miss! for the most authentic tortillas you can get your hands on. (56A Manor Street, Stoneybatter, D7, Tel: (01) 670 7799, sabormex@indigo.ie, open daily, Lunch €)

● **101 Talbot** The cult 101 has some of the choicest vegetarian cooking in the capital: three bean chilli burritos with fennel and coriander sauce; marinated tomato and feta crostini; baba gnu served with pitta and crudités; roast vegetable and walnut strudel; parsnip and hazelnut cakes with spiced aubergine purée. The room has an energy like no other, so it's always party time in 101. Great service and great value. (101 Talbot Street, Dublin 1, Tel: (01) 874 5011, Fax: (01) 875 5011 Open: 5pm-11pm Tue-Sat, Dinner €€€)

● **Osborne Restaurant** Stefan Matz is one of Ireland's finest cooks, and has been working at the Osborne for some time now, way out Northside at the Portmarnock Hotel. Mr Matz has always been an assured and sympathetic cook for vegetarians, with his pasta dishes, in particular, having no peer. (Portmarnock Hotel, Strand Road, Portmarnock, Tel: (01) 846 0611 www.portmarnock.com)

● **Soup Dragon** Sometimes they serve the soups too hot in here, but that's about the only mistake the girls make in the Dragon, a tiny (and perpetually jammed) little soup station at the river-end of Capel Street. Smart, funky food, and great value. (168 Capel St, D1, Tel: (01) 872 3277, Open Lunch €)

● **The Vaults D1** This enormous, groovy pub is sports-themed, and has loads of big screens, but thanks to owner Michael Martin, the food isn't a second-team stringer, and the pastas and pizzas are smartly delivered and worth your attention even if you can't tell the difference between Robbie and Roy Keane. (Harbourmaster Place, Dublin 1, Tel: (01) 605 4700 www.thevaults.ie)

CITY CENTRE

● **Avoca** A beautiful room on the third floor is the
city outpost of Avoca, and once you
can drag yourself away from the
desirable collectibles, the food is ace;
field mushroom and Parmesan tartlet;
roasted pepper stew with chevre
croute; pea asparagus and herb risotto.
Real cool crowd, fab atmosphere.
(Suffolk St, D2, Tel: (01) 677 4215 www.avoca.ie Open
Lunch €€)

● **Bang Café** Lorcan Gribbin's cooking
has set Bang to rights: plum tomato
and goat's cheese galettes; pumpkin
gnocchi with artichoke and
mushroom salad; char-grilled
vegetable salad; linguini of wild
mushrooms. The banquette is too low, the
buzz is mighty.
(11 Merrion Row, Dublin 2, Tel: (01) 676 0898, Fax:
676 0899 www.bangrestaurant.com Open 12.30pm-
3pm Mon-Sat, 6pm-10.30pm Mon-Wed, 6pm-11pm
Thu-Sat. Lunch €, Dinner €€€)

● **Cornucopia** Deirdre McCafferty's Cornucopia is
still packing them in after all these years,
and whilst this pioneering vegetarian
wholefood destination might not
deliver any surprises, its loyal
following is a testament to its
enduring appeal. The generous, filling
and unprententious food is served from a
counter; and daily specials such as chickpea balti
come with a choice of two fresh salads, at keen
prices. There is an extensive list of freshly squeezed
juices and smoothies, again very reasonably priced.
(19 Wicklow St, D2, Tel: (01) 677 7583. Open Lunch &
early Dinner, Meals €-€€)

● **Ely** Everyone's favourite wine bar has a stonkingly wonderful selection of wines, including many which are available by the glass and which will persuade you to linger long time in these intimate clubby rooms no matter what time of day it is. Whilst the food choice is limited, don't miss the splendid cheeses from Sheridan brothers and some nifty bruschetta. (22 Ely Place, D2, Tel: (01) 676 8986. Open Lunch €€ and Dinner €€)

● **L'Ecrivain** Derry Clarke and his team run the city's sharpest, most admired restaurant, and the vegetarian cooking is as sublime as everything else: crisp wrap of goat's cheese with pine nuts, pickled vegetables and beetroot jam; baked stuffed cannelloni with roast root vegetables, spiced cauliflower, red pepper and tomato sauce; leek tartlet with saffron dressing and tossed leaves. Unquestionably Dubliners' favourite restaurant.
(109 Lower Baggot Street, Dublin 2, Tel: (01) 661 1919, Fax: 661 0617, enquiries@lecrivain.com www.lecrivain.com Open: 12.30pm-2pm Mon-Fri, 7pm-11pm Mon-Sat, Lunch €€€, Dinner €€€€€)

● **Fresh Café** This reliable vegetarian day-time provider has a dedicated lunchtime audience who enjoy vegetarian cooking that is wholesome, but could profitably enjoy a little more chutzpah and daring. Sandwiches and salads are consistent, and are abetted by daily specials such as lentil and spinach dhansak. Stout desserts such as carrot cake are good, and juices are ready-made and poured from the fridge.
(Powerscourt Townhouse Centre, Clarendon St, D2, Tel: (01) 671 9669. Open daily Mon-Sat, until 8pm Thurs, Lunch €€)

● **Jacob's Ladder** Adrian Roche is one of the city's best, and most thoughtful cooks. His light and assured touch animates dishes such as spiced tomato soup with ratatouille, or Thai spiced vegetables with couscous, glazed shallots and wild mushroom fumé. Lovely views out across Trinity, if you can take your eyes off the food. (4-5 Nassau St, D2, Tel: (01) 670 3865, Fax: 670 3868, www.jacobsladder.ie, Open 12.30pm-2.30pm, 6pm-10.30pm Tue-Sat. Lunch €€ & Dinner €€€)

● **Juice** David Keane's Juice is a light high-ceilinged room with a nice relaxed, friendly feel. Among the savouries for lunch, half a dozen light meals and the same number of mains provide a wide-ranging global selection. The antipasti plate has excellent baba ganoush and tabbouleh, while a vegetable and tofu stir-fry with coconut served with some nicely cooked wholegrain rice is excellent. The desserts are very fine, and the juices and smoothies are superb. (South Gt Georges St, D2, Tel: (01) 457 7856)

SOUTHSIDE DUBLIN

● **Crema** Everyone comes to Crema for their famous soups, but there are lots and lots of vegetarian choices on a menu heavily tilted in favour of smart vegetarian cooking. (312 Lwr Rathmines Rd, D6, Tel: (01) 496 5555. Open Lunch €€)

● **Dish** Beloved of brunchers, Dish is one of the key southside rooms. Butternut squash risotto is great, hummus with chick pea relish and Lebanese bread judged just right; and don't miss those cocktails. Dish's sister room – Tribeca in Ranelagh – is just as hip, just as hot, just as busy. (146 Upper Leeson St, Dublin 4, Tel: (01) 664 2135, Fax: 664 2136 Open: noon-4pm, 6pm-11pm Mon-Sun, Lunch €€, Dinner €€€€)

● **O'Connell's** The vegetarian choices can seem token – grilled garlic and parsley bread with pesto; organic omelette with pepper, courgette and sweet chilli sauce; bruschetta of flat mushrooms – but the excellent ingredients used more than compensate for the small choice in this pulsing brasserie. (Bewley's Aparthotel, Merrion Rd, Ballsbridge, Dublin 4, Tel: (01) 647 3304, Fax: 647 3499, oconnellsballsbridge@eircom.net www.oconnellsballsbridge.com Open: 7am-10.30am, 12.30pm-2.30pm, 6pm-10.30pm Mon-Sat (Sat from 7.30am), 8am-11am, 12.30pm-3pm, 6pm-9.30pm Sun, Lunch €€, Dinner €€€)

● **Roly's Bistro** The most energised room in the entire city is raucously loud, and unmissable for any visitor. Paul Cartwright's cooking is right on the money: fine roast vegetable salad with roast garlic dressing; tomato and rocket risotto; mushroom and blue cheese ravioli, and don't miss the excellent gluten-free bread they sell. (7 Ballsbridge Terrace, Ballsbridge, D4, Tel: (01) 668 2611, Fax: 660 8535 rolysbistro@ireland.com, www.rolysbistro.com, Open Lunch, €€€ & Dinner €€€€)

● **Tribeca** Ranelagh's cult address, and one of the most difficult places in town to get a table. The house salad is always excellent, the noodles are excellent, the spaghetti alla Norma right on the money. Great sounds, and brilliant for brunch at the weekends. (65 Ranelagh Village, Dublin 6, Tel: (01) 497 4174, Fax: 4911584, Open: 8.30am-11.30am Mon-Fri, noon-11pm Mon-Sun, Meals €-€€€)

● **The Expresso Bar and Café** The same fine pastas and salads you will find in the IFSC are here also, and the Expresso is a very popular brunch destination. (St Mary's Rd, Ballsbridge, Tel: (01) 660 0585, Open daily, Lunch €, & Dinner €)

● **The Gotham Café** Good pizzas are the main attraction and account for the perennial popularity of the Gotham (5 Sth Anne St, D2. Tel: (01) 679 5266. Open Lunch & Dinner, Meals €-€€)

TEMPLE BAR

Il Baccaro
a little slice of Naples in a basement wine bar at the corner of Meetinghouse Square, which provides some of the best fun to be had in the capital – just don't drink too much of that interestingly rustic wine they serve. Yeah, it is 3am already. (Tel: (01) 671 4597, Open evenings €€)

Bar Italia
a slice of Torino at the edge of Temple Bar, where you get real Italian cooking from Stefano Crescenzi – great pastas, paninis, and you can even order the minestrone with confidence, and – don't miss this! – what may be the finest espresso in the city. Great place.
(Tel: (01) 679 5128, Open Lunch. €)

Eden
the service is too opinionated, but Eden is otherwise a good, grown-up restaurant and also serves some of the very best cocktails in the city.
(Tel: (01) 670 5372., Open Lunch & Dinner €€-€€€)

The Chameleon
a simple and genuine restaurant with a distinctive style of Indonesian food and great service.
(Tel: (01) 671 0362, Open Dinner €€)

The Elephant & Castle
The E&C is not as sharp as it was during the 90's, but this Temple Bar powerhouse remains as popular as ever. (18 Temple Bar, D2, Tel: (01) 679 3121 Open all day. €€)

Gruel
Soup-kitchen sister of the Mermaid, with fab cooking. (67 Dame Street, D2. Tel: (01) 670 7119. Open daily Mon-Sun. Meals €-€€)

The Mermaid Café
Ben Gorman's Dame Street restaurant is one of the city's great addresses and produces true, original and mega-tasty cooking – artichoke and cannelloni bean compote; aubergine and red pepper and goat's cheese compote, some fantastic bruschetta and awesome Bloody Marys! Brilliant brunch. (Dame Street, D2, Tel: (01) 670 8236 Open Lunch & Dinner €€)

Queen of Tarts
Head here if you have a sweet tooth, for the Queen's tarts are regarded as amongst the very finest in the city. (Cork Hill, D2, Tel: (01) 670 7499. Open daily. Lunch €)

Sonar Gaon
A fantastically diverse vegetarian menu includes masala dosais, crispy crepes of rice and lentils stuffed with spiced potatoes, Don't miss the golgappa and the other street food specialities. (6 Crow Street, Tel: (01) 672 8822 sonargaon@eircom.net Open 7 days from 5pm, Dinner €€)

The Tea Room
Anthony Ely does some of the city's loveliest cooking: mozzarella with spiced aubergine compote and rucola; panko breaded goat's cheese with green bean salad, making this gorgeous room a true cutting-edge space. (The Clarence Hotel, 6-8 Wellington Quay, D2, Tel: (01) 670 9000. Open Lunch & Dinner €€€)

WINE DESTINATIONS

● **Bond** See the entry for the restaurant, but you don't have to eat to stop here and pick up a bottle from the brilliant collection in the basement shop. (5 Beresford Place, Dublin 1, Tel: (01) 855 9244 Fax: 888 1612, info@bond.ie www.BOND.ie Open: noon-3pm Mon-Fri, 6pm-9pm Mon-Wed, 6pm-10pm Sat. Closed Sun. Lunch €€, Dinner €€€)

● **Berry Bros & Rudd** The most beautiful wine shop in the city, filled with beautiful wines. Downstairs is the pricey stuff if your ship comes in, but don't overlook their own label wines which are modest and pleasing, not least their always enjoyable claret. (4 Harry St, D2, Tel: (01) 677 3444)

● **Burgundy Direct** Conor Richardson's bespoke company is a must-know for those addicted to Pinot Noir. (8 Monaloe Way, Blackrock, Tel: (01) 289 6615, Fax: (01) 289 8470, burgundy@indigo.ie)

● **Cabot & Co** One of the newcomers to the wine scene, Liam and Sinead Cabot's fine shop is a great address for cult Aussie and Italian wines. (Valentia House, Custom House Square IFSC, D1, Tel: (01) 636 0616, sales@cabotandco.com)

● **Dunne & Crescenzi** D&C is virtually a one-stop shop for the choicest Italian comestibles and speciality foods, but don't overlook the excellent range of Italian wines you will find here and nowhere else, and do have a glass with some anti pasti as you choose. (14 Sth Frederick St, D2, Tel: (01) 677 3815, crescenz@iol.ie)

● **Findlater's** The Findlater's shop is not a great space to browse in, but the list is always 24-carat impressive. (The Harcourt St Vaults, 10 Upr Hatch St, D2, Tel: (01) 475 1699, sales@findlaters.com)

● **Layden Fine Wines** The wine shop of the brilliant Epicurean Mall has a fine selection, and great service. (Epicurean Food Hall, Lwr Liffey St, D1, Tel: (01) 878 2221 laydenfinewines.com)

● **McCabe's** A truly great wine shop, with great classes for beginners and really brilliant service. (51-55 Mount Merrion Ave, Blackrock, Co Dublin, Tel: (01) 288 2037, Fax: (01) 288 3447, mccabeswines.com)

● **Michael's Wines** A smart, friendly local wine store in comfy Mount Merrion with a sharply independent array of wines. (63 Deerpark Road, Mount Merrion, Tel: (01) 278 0377 michael.lowe@oceanfree.net)

● **Mitchell's** A second branch out in Glasthule complements this fine, venerable city centre institution. A gentlemanly address, yes, but never snobbish or self-conscious, and the wines are ace. (21 Kildare St, D2, Tel: (01) 676 0766 mitchellandson.com, mitchkst@indigo.ie)

● **O'Brien's Wines** This energetic chain has branches all over the southside and has been one of the most dynamic wine companies in the capital in recent years (30-32 Donnybrook Rd, D4, Tel: (01) 269 3139, Fax: (01) 269 3033, obrienswines.ie)

● **Oddbins** There is also an enormous Oddbins store in the Blanchardstown shopping centre, and whilst the selection of wines in all the shops is always impressive, it is a major ordeal to buy a case in Baggot Street or Blackrock, and help is rarely forthcoming from the staff. Inconveniences aside, the selection is artful. (17 Upper Baggot St, D4, Tel: (01) 667 3033; 23 Rock Hill, Blackrock, Co Dublin, Tel: (01) 278 3844; 125 Braemor Rd, Churchtown, D14, Tel: (01) 296 3111; 360 Clontarf Rd, D3, Tel: (01) 833 1653; www.oddbins.com)

Searson's of Monkstown Quirky, idiosyncratic and inspiring. Frank and Charles Searson's shop has great everyday wines, and the best en primeur offers in the country. (Monkstown Crescent, Tel: (01) 280 0405, Fax: (01) 280 4771, info@searsons.com)

Terroirs Gorgeous shop with gorgeous foods alongside gorgeous wines. Sure, prices can be steep, but Terroirs is a specialist shop, the Savile Row of wine shops, though there are some choice bargains to be had alongside the stellar wines. (103 Morehampton Rd, D4, Tel: (01) 667 1311, Fax: 667 1312, terroirs.ie)

Vaughan Johnson VJ is a specialist in South African wines, and one of the key Temple Bar addresses. Go go for those Chenins! (Essex Street East, Temple Bar Tel: (01) 671 5355)

The Vintry Evelyn Jones' shop may be petite, but it's jammed with great wines and is an archetype of the informed independent wine shop. (102 Rathgar Road, D6, Tel: (01) 490 5477

SERIOUS BREWS

• Beer lovers should not miss the superb beers brewed in Smithfield by the Dublin Brewing Co. Just try a cool bottle of Maeve's Crystal Wheat, and all your troubles dissipate and disappear in a moment of beer bliss. Their organic cider is pretty mighty stuff too.

• The Porterhouse on Parliament Street is not just a pub: it is a place of pilgrimage for beer lovers. What's your favourite? Wrassler's XXXX will do us nicely, thanks very much.

• And there are some nice brews also in Messrs Maguire, a big busy pub just at O'Connell Bridge.

10 USEFUL
WINE WEBSITES

1
WWW.BUBBLEBROTHERS.COM

2
WWW.BESTCELLARS.IE

3
WWW.DIRECTWINE.CO.UK

4
WWW.EWINE.IE

5
WWW.FINDLATERS.COM

6
WWW.JNWINE.COM

7
WWW.ONTHECASE.IE

8
WWW.SEARSONS.COM

9
WWW.THEWINEROOM.IE

10
WWW.WINES-DIRECT.COM

THE BEST FOR JUICES AND SMOOTHIES

Itsabagel
Organic fruit and vegetable juices, and homemade lemonade. (Epicurean Mall, D1, Tel: (01) 874 0486; Dun Laoghaire Pavilion, itsabagel.com)

The Joose Bar
Invent your own city squeeze. (7a Poolbeg St, D2, Tel: (01) 679 9611 Fax: 01-679 9642, www.joosebar.com)

Juice
The original of the species. (South St Georges St, D2, Tel: 01 475 7856)

The Milk Bar
Ace juices and really sharp food. (Montague St, Tel: (01) 478 8450)

Nectar
The carrot and ginger will cure any hangover. (53 Ranelagh Village, D6, Tel: (01) 491 0934)

Nude
The best smoothies, and don't miss the wheatgrass shots. (21 Suffolk St, D2, Tel: (01) 672 5577, also Go Nude on Lower Leeson Street)

ETHNIC RESTAURANTS

● **AYA** Yoichi Hoashi's little chain of sushi bars – you will find Aya also in Donnybrook and the IFSC – are fun places, great for hanging out and downing a few beers as well as their spirited modern Japanese cooking. (rere Brown Thomas, Clarendon Street, D2, Tel: (01) 677 1544 mail@aya.ie. aya.ie. Open Lunch & Dinner. Meals €-€€)

● **The Bombay Pantry** This humungously busy shop – don't turn up and expect food in 5 minutes! – serves some of the best Indian vegetarian specialities you can find on the southside, and has been consistently impressive over the years. A second branch in Rathmines now keeps city folk happy.

(Glenageary Shopping Centre, Tel: (01) 285 6683. 14 Rathgar Road, Rathmines, Tel: (01) 496 9695. Open Lunch & Dinner. Meals €)

● **Mao** The Chatham Street Mao now has a fellow-traveller branch at the Pavilion in Dun Laoghaire. Neither serves authentic Oriental food, but they are fun rooms and the vegetarian choices are good: spring rolls with tofu and shiitake; gado gado; vegetable hokkien; red pumpkin curry.

(2/3 Chatham Row, D2, Tel: (01) 670 4899, Fax: 670 4999; The Pavilion, Dun Laoghaire Seafront, Tel: (01) 214 8090, cafemao.com. Open Lunch & Dinner, Meals €€)

● **Montys of Katmandu**
The cult Temple Bar destination has the swishest, most authentic Nepalese cooking you can find, with vegetable versions of all their main generic dishes shown appropriate respect, as well as a section devoted to vegetarian dishes: navartna curry; their excellent paneer served with masala sauce and in a dry kerau style, and the breads, rice and side dishes are worth the trip all on their own.

(28 Eustace St, Temple Bar, Dublin 2, Tel: (01) 670 4911, Fax: 494 4359, montys@eircom.net www.montys.ie Open: Noon-2.30pm, 6pm-11.30pm Mon-Sat, 6pm-11pm Sun, Menus from €€€)

● **The Olive Tree** Bahaa Jaafi's restaurant fuses the cuisines of the central Mediterranean with impressive skill, and there are always lots of intriguing and well-realised choices.(22 Newtownpark Avenue, Blackrock, Tel: (01) 278 0933)

● **Poppadom Restaurant** Poppadom is widely regarded as offering some of the most interesting Indian cooking in the city, and Xerxes Ginwalla also runs one of the very best rooms. There is a real thrill in their kathiawari chhena – goat's cheese thepla shortbread – the navratan korma, the kovalam vegetables, and the excellent nans and rice dishes. Don't miss the tak-a-tin speciality at their Newlands Cross takeaway, another vital address with great cooking. (01- 4 1111 44) (91a Rathgar Road, Dublin 6, Tel: (01) 490 2383, Fax: 492 3900, Open: 6pm-midnight Mon-Sun, Dinner €€€)

● **Shalimar** Shalimar was one of the first Indian restaurants in the city, and has a devoted clientele. The vegetarian choices are fairly typical – onion bhaji, shabnami paneer; kaju korma; malai kofta – but the cooking is precise, and the room is very busy at weekends. (17 South Gt Georges St, D2, Tel: (01) 671 0738, Fax: 677 3478, shalimar@iol.ie, Open Lunch, €€ & Dinner €€€)

● **Sichuan Restaurant** This beloved Chinese restaurant has always had a strong vegetarian following, thanks in part to some very excellent dishes with bean curd. Friendly service also, but make sure to book at weekends, when the place is packed out with happy southside families. (4 Lwr Kilmacud Rd, Stillorgan, Co Dublin, Tel: (01) 288 4871, Fax: 288 0882, Open Lunch €€ and Dinner €€€)

● **Tulsi** Tulsi has a number of branches in Dublin and throughout the country, and whilst the enormous list is initially alienating, with innumerable variations of every dish, the vegetarian selection is typically strong, and value for money is keen. (17a Lower Baggot Street, Dublin 2, Tel: (01) 676 4578)

● **Vermillion** Nisheeth Tak's newest venture is one of the hot spots in Terenure, a lovely room with some provocative and creative Indian cooking that is making quite a splash. (94/96 Terenure Rd Nth, D6W, Tel: (01) 499 1400 www.vermilion.ie)

● **Wagamama** The Dublin branch is the best of this small chain of Japanese restaurants, with very fine noodles and a cool school of design that we just adore. (Sth King St, D2, Tel: (01) 478 2152. Open L&D. Meals €-€€)

● **Yamamori Noodles** A good, fun room with some nice spicy noodles that are just the thing with chilled wine. (71 Sth Gt George's St, D2, Tel: (01) 475 5001. Open L&D. Meals €-€€)

ETHNIC SHOPS

The area around Parnell Street and Moore Street in D1 has been excitingly colonised by many new ethnic shops. Look out for John Bankole's Tropical Store on Parnell Street. Joyceanna on Moore Street; Slavyanskaya Lavka, which specialises in Baltic and Russian foods. Azure Holdings is for Chinese foods and there are many other stalls selling ethnic foods in the Moore Street indoor market. In the centre of the city, The Asia Market on Drury Street is still the best ethnic store in the city, the place where you will find everything Asian that can be used for cooking and eating, from woks to bak choi, from noodles of many hues. There is also the Asian Food Store on Camden Street. The Islamic Centre on South Circular Road also has a store selling specialist foods. For Japanese and Pacific rim cooking, then AYA at the rere of Brown Thomas on Clarendon Street has a good selection of ethnic foods for sale in its shop, so if you are determined to make sushi, start here. The newest branches - AYA 2 Go in Donnybrook and the AYA Deli in the IFSC in the financial quarter – also sell some specialist foods as well as food-to-go.

GREAT CITY HOTELS

● **The Clarence Hotel and The Tea Room**
Classic, ageless style, high prices, great cooking. (6-8 Wellington Quay, Dublin 2, Tel: (01) 407 0800, Fax: 407 0820, reservations@theclarence.ie, www.theclarence.ie (Open all year, breakfast, lunch and dinner, Lunch €€€€, Dinner €€€€€, Rates €€€)

● **The Clarion** The Synergie restaurant could be sharper, but we like the lean, colourful style of the The Clarion, and the location close to the river is great. (IFSC, Dublin 1, Tel: (01) 433 8800, Fax: 433 8811, info@clarionhotelifsc.com www.clarionhotelifsc.com Open: all year, Rates €€€)

● **The Morrison Hotel** Ultra hip in every way, with great cooking in Halo. (Ormond Quay, Dublin 1, Tel: (01) 887 2421, Fax: 878 3185 info@morrisonhotel.ie www.morrisonhotel.ie Open all year: Lunch €€€, Dinner €€€€€, Rooms €€€)

● **The Morgan** They have finally sorted out the ground floor bar – the Morgan Bar – and whilst street noise is a factor here (it's smack on Fleet Street in Temple Bar) the moody rooms in The Morgan are stylish and intimate. (10 Fleet St, D2, Tel: (01) 679 3939 Fax: 679 3946 sales@themorgan.com www.themorgan.com Rooms €€€)

SHOPPING

CITY CENTRE
· · · · · · · · · · · · · · · ·

● **Avoca Handweavers** Head downstairs
to the basement for beautifully
packaged treats, sourced with great
skill. Good food-to-go at lunchtime
also. (Suffolk St, D2, Tel: (01) 677 4215
avoca.ie)

● **The Big Cheese Co.** Great cheese selection
plus very interesting speciality foods you simply won't
find anywhere else. (Trinity St, D2, Tel: (01) 671 1399)

● **Crème de la Crème** Fabulous
patisserie which leaves every other
sweet thing in Dublin in the shade.
(Epicurean Food Mall, D1, Tel: (01)
836 4202)

● **Dunne & Crescenzi** Great Italian
specialities, specially grains and
pulses and good oils. (14 Sth
Frederick St, D2, Tel: (01) 677 3815)

● **The Gallic Kitchen** The nicest
savoury baking in the city, with great
pies and tarts. Also at the Saturday
market in Temple Bar. (49 Francis St,
D8, Tel: (01) 454 4912)

● **The Good Food Store** A beautifully
simple, elegant shop, which in addition
to selling superb organic produce also
packs 'em in at lunchtime for great
food-to-go. (7 Pembroke Lane, D4,
Tel: (01) 667 5656, Ringsend (01) 668
4514)

● **Laragh Stuart Foods** Lovely prepared foods, cooked with real verve and imagination and no little style. (George's St Arcade, D2, Tel: (01) 617 4827)

● **Listons** Karen Liston's shop is a smashing deli that enjoys a real neighbourhood feel. Great salads, sarnies and choice foods from pulses to wines, cheeses to breads, are sold with knowledge and enthusiasm, just the sort of thing Camden Street needs. (25 Lower Camden Street, D2, Tel: (01) 405 4779, listonsfood@eircom.net)

● **Magills** Kim Condon's shop is one of the original delis, and still as good as ever. Check out the Stone Oven breads and excellent cheeses. (14 Clarendon St, D2, Tel: (01) 671 3830)

● **La Maison des Gourmets** Expensive French prepared foods, cooked with meticulous care. The breads are particularly interesting. (15 Castle Market, D2, Tel: (01) 672 7258)

● **The Olive Green Food Co** A brilliant little food stall with masses of interesting, must-have-it! foods. (George's St Arcade, D2, olivegreen@indigo.ie)

● **Sheridan's Cheesemongers** Sheridan's is one of the city's pivotal addresses, not just for superlative cheeses in superlative condition sold by superlatively knowledgeable staff, but also for many other fantastic artisan foods, many of them imported direct from Italy. (11 Sth Anne St, D2, Tel: (01) 679 3143, sheridanscheesemongers@eircom.net)

● **Temple Bar Bakery** Head here for some nice domestic-style baking. (Essex Street West, Tel: (01) 672 9882)

SOUTHSIDE

• **Blackrock**
Cakes & Co. The sugarcraft these women weave is so fine that it can seem that the cakes are purely decorative, but they are also quite delicious. (25 Rock Hill, Blackrock Village, Tel: (01) 283 6544)

• **Donnybrook**
Donnybrook Fair is a smart deli-meets-supermarket in the manner of Harvey Nick's 5th Floor. Interesting design makes for a great shopping space. (Morehampton Rd, Tel: (01) 668 3556)

Grainne Murphy's Douglas Food Co is a fine traiteur, but also a key address for people with special dietary needs, who are carefully looked after. A second shop in Dalkey is on Castle Street. (53 Donnybrook Rd, D4, Tel: (01) 269 4066; 14 Castle St, Dalkey, Tel: (01) 284 7184 grainne@thedouglasfoodco.ie)

Roy Fox. One of the greatest treats in Dublin is to spend a weekend hour browsing and buying in this fantastic shop. They appear to sell – literally! – everything. (49a Main St, Donnybrook, Tel: (01) 269 2892)

Terroirs sells fabulous wines along with great imported speciality foods. You seek pumpkin oil? They have it. (103 Morehampton Rd, D4, Tel: (01) 667 1311, Fax: 667 1312, terroirs.ie)

• **Dundrum**
The Mulberry Market is an excellent market shop packed with lots of good things. (Airfield House, Upper Kilmacud Road, Dundrum, D14, Tel: (01) 296 0212)

• **Ranelagh, Rathmines & Rathgar**
A Taste of Italy is great for dried Italian goods and other rarities, and check out the bread. (37 Dunville Ave, D6, Tel: (01) 497 3411)

Morton's is one of the best-loved supermarkets on the southside, with charming service and a true independent spirit. (15 Dunville Ave, D6, Tel: (01) 497 1254)

Redmond's is a great wine shop and a good deli, with spirited, friendly service from the team.
(25 Ranelagh Village, D6, Tel: (01) 496 0552)

Fothergills sells some of the nicest sweet baking you can find, served by dedicated, delightful folk.
 (141 Upper Rathmines Rd, D6, Tel: (01) 496 2511)

NORTHSIDE

• Clontarf
Nolan's is a vital little supermarket which manages to have just the things you need.
(49 Vernon Ave, D3, Tel: (01) 833 6929)

• Malahide
The Foodware Store is a bustling emporium with really imaginative salads and other foods-to-go. A key northside address. (19 Old Street, Malahide, Tel: (01) 845 1830)

• D7 & Stoneybatter
Lime and Lemongrass is a tiny shop just off Capel Street packed with groovy relishes, sauces, dips and oils.
(2-3 Mary's Abbey, D7, Tel: (01) 872 2965 lemongrass@eircom.net limeandlemongrass.com)

Little Italy is great for dried porcini, pasta, arborio and decent inexpensive wines.
 (North King St, D7, Tel: (01) 872 5208)

MARKETS

● The Temple Bar Market

In a few short years, the Temple Bar Saturday Market has blossomed into one of the city's don't miss it! destinations. The number of producers selling at the market in Meetinghouse Square has grown steadily, and the sense of camaraderie amongst the traders is as great an attraction as the fantastic foods they sell. If you haven't toured the market and snapped up goodies hither and thither, you haven't done Dublin.

(Open 9am-6pm each Saturday)

● The Cow's Lane Market

This brand new venture in the Old City has been set up by Temple Bar Properties to concentrate on suppliers of raw ingredients. Some of the initial producers include: Marc Michel's Organic Life and Denis Healy's organic vegetables, both from County Wicklow, and there are more fantastic organics from Absolutely Organic. Mary MacRory has organic strawberries in season, whilst the Abbey Cheese Co from County Laois has cheeses and clever preserved cheeses for salads, all organic.

(Cow's Lane, Temple Bar, 9am-6pm Saturday)

● The Dublin Food Co-Op

You can't beat the DFC-O for peerless organic and biodynamic vegetables, for a marvellous agit-prop atmosphere, and for vital wholefoods. Mighty craic. nb: Look out for a possible change of location soon. (St Andrew's Centre, Pearse St, Tel: (01) 873 0451, 9.30am-3pm Saturday)

County
Galway

GALWAY CITY
● ● ● ● ● ● ● ● ● ● ● ● ● ●

EATING

● **Delight** A terrific little café with smart food to go and excellent treats in store; don't miss the Illy coffee and the hot rolls. (Upper Abbeygate St, Tel: (091) 567823, Open Lunch €)

● **Goya's** The best baker in the west is how they talk about Emer Murray, but it's not just the sweet things that are delectable: everything in Goya's is superb, cooked with love and care. (Kirwan's Lane, Tel: (091) 567010 Open daily, €)

● **Nimmo's** The supremely Bohemian nature of Galway is best expressed in Nimmo's, a lovably whacky space that pulses with life. The cooking is excellent, the wines superb, the atmosphere inimitable. An essential part of the city. (Nimmo's Restaurant, Spanish Arch, Galway, Tel: (091) 561114 Open: 12.30pm-3pm, 6.60pm-10pm Tue-Sun. Wine bar open all day, from 6pm Sun. Lunch €€, Dinner €€€)

● **The River God Café** Some find it a little spicy, but the cooking has some genuine moments in this busy upstairs room in the centre of town. (Quay St, Tel: (091) 565811 Open Lunch €€ & Dinner €€€)

STAYING

● **Devon Dell** DD is a simple house, but Berna Kelly looks after her guests in such an elemental, maternal way that you can't wait to get back to Salthill. (47 Devon Park, Lower Salthill, Galway, Tel: (091) 528306 devondell@iol.ie www.devondell.com Open: February-October, Rates €€)

● **Norman Villa** Design heaven, and one of the most hospitable houses in the country, thanks to the amazing energy of Mark and Dee Keogh. (86 Lower Salthill, Tel & Fax: (091) 521131 normanvilla@oceanfree.net www.normanvilla.com Open: March-31 October, Rates €€)

SHOPPING

● **Galway Saturday Morning Market** This is still the best street market in Ireland, a magical experience that shows Galway at its beautiful best. (Saturday morning, around St Nicholas' Church)

● **Healthwise** Aidan Kelly's store is one of the longest established wholefood shops in the country, almost a quarter century old! (5 Lower Abbeygate St, Galway, Tel: (091) 568761)

● **McCambridges** One of Galway's shopping institutions, still as nimble and surprising as ever. (Shop St, Galway, Tel: (091) 562259)

● **The Noble Vine** Noel O'Loughlen's selection of wines is amongst the most singular in the country. (Terryland, Tel: (091) 565749 noblevine@eircom.net)

● **Riverville Farmhouse Cheese** Robbie and Anne Gannon's excellent cheeses are amongst the newest of the farmhouse cheeses, but they already have several awards under their belt. Look out for the smoked cheese and the flavoured varieties as well as the plain Riverville. (Craughwell, Tel: (091) 848232)

● **Sheridans Cheesemongers** The Galway branch of the peerless cheesemongers, and unmissable for thrilling foods, and really exciting food-to-go. (Castle Street, Galway, Tel: (091) 564829)

● **The Vineyard** Muriel Kineen's fine shop is a vital address for hunting down good bottles of wine in the city. (Mainguard Street, Tel: (091) 561816)

CONNEMARA AND THE ARAN ISLANDS

The Connemara Hamper
This is the best shop in Clifden, hell, in Connemara!
(Clifden, Tell: (095) 21054 abaco@iol.ie)

Mainistir House Hostel.
Unique hostel with delicious vegetarian cooking.
(Kilronan, Tel: (099) 61169, Fax: 61351, Rates €)

The Quay House
Paddy and Julia Foyle's gorgeous house is the choicest address in busy Clifden (Beach Road, Clifden, Tel: (095) 21369, Fax: 21608 thequay@iol.ie www.thequayhouse.com Open: Mid Mar-Early-Nov, Rates €€€)

Seaview House
A pretty and hospitable B&B just down from the square.
(Clifden, Connemara, Tel: (095) 21441 sgriffin@eircom.net www.connemara.net/seaview Open: Open all year, except Christmas, Rates €€)

County
Kerry

north

east

west

south

EATING

● **Sheen Falls Lodge** Chris Farrell has propelled the cooking in the glamorous Sheen Falls Lodge into the stratosphere in recent times, and some of his finest and most acute creativity is reserved for the vegetarian menu prepared each evening. Fresh tagliarini with onion purée, French tarragon and plum tomato confit, or a light tomato and cucumber jelly with horseradish cream and wild asparagus, shows the sort of intense intent he can summon, whilst truffle and herb risotto with baby navette and beurre noisette, or pea mousseline with fondant potato and lentilles du Puy mix the gutsy with the serene. It's expensive, it's formal, and it's absolutely great. (Kenmare, Tel: (064) 41600 Fax: (064) 41386 info@sheenfallslodge.ie www.sheenfallslodge.ie Open Dinner. Closed Jan, Dinner €€€€€, Rooms €€€)

● **Deenagh Lodge** A surprise to find Indian Thali plates in the gatehouse to Killarney National Park? Sure is. Joan Greene draws on her travels in India to produce well-loved vegetarian cooking in this beautiful old gate lodge. Sit outside on a summer's day enjoying her legendary soups and salads. (National Park, Tel: (064) 36274 Open Lunch, €-€€)

STAYING

● **Iskeroon** Iskeroon is a house that takes your breath away. It's in an absurdly impossible and ridiculously romantic setting, and it's an utterly beautiful house, and leaving it is simply heartbreaking. One of the real cult addresses in Ireland. (Bunavalla, Caherdaniel, Tel: (066) 94 75119 Fax: 9475488 info@iskeroon.com www.iskeroon.com Open May-September, Rooms €€)

● **The Killarney Park Hotel** The Killarney Park is one of the best-run hotels in Ireland, and typical of the care Donagh Davern and his team exhibit is the fact that they prepare a special vegetarian menu every evening. It's smart, sharp cooking; deep-fried bon bons of Boilie goat's cheese with tapenade dressing; cream of parsnip soup with truffle oil; risotto of garden vegetables with home-dried tomatoes, and fine salads and desserts make for energising food that is as crisply delivered as everything else in this exceptional hotel. The food in the bar offers fewer choices, but is also beautifully accomplished. (Kenmare Place, Killarney, Tel: (064) 35555, Fax: 35266, info@killarneyparkhotel.ie www.killarneyparkhotel.ie Open all year, except Christmas, Rooms €€€)

● **Shelburne Lodge** Maura Foley's gorgeous house is sensationally sensual, a dream address for style lovers who exult in the remarkable design savvy of this inspiring woman. Beautiful breakfasts bring a stay here to a delirious crescendo. Don't miss it. (Killowen, Cork Road, Kenmare, Tel: (064) 41013, Fax: 42135, Open1 April-30 October, Rooms €€)

ORGANICS IN KERRY

Billy Clifford
Billy farms an idyllically pretty little patch of land out on the Cork road out of Kenmare, and keeps most of the good cooks in town happy with excellent organic produce. (Kenmare, Tel: (064) 41693)

Gorthbrack Organic Farm
Contact Ian McGrigor for details of his box delivery system of organic vegetables. (Gorthbrack, Tel: (066) 37042)

Miltown Organic Market
Saturday morning is the time to turn up for Mary O'Riordan's smart little organic market, which also features many local crafts. (The Natural Home Garden & Farm Centre is open Tue-Sat, Tel: (066) 976 7869)

Mary Pawle Wines Mary Pawle's company was the first to specialise in organic wines, and has become one of the key specialist wine companies in the country. The list is particularly strong on Spain, but Mary has a skill at searching out exciting wines in areas where you least expect them. (Gortamullen, Kenmare, Tel: (064) 41443)

SHOPPING

● **An Grianan** Elaine Avery's shop is where you go for health and wholefoods in Dingle. (Dykegate Lane, Dingle (066) 51910)

● **Dingle Peninsula Cheese** Maya Binder's cheeses have built a cult following for their powerful flavourfulness and creativity. The Dilliskus cheese is flavoured with seaweed (Ms Binder's partner, fact fans, is the gifted Olivier Beaujouan, whose seaweed specialities are great treats), and the plain Benoskee is stunning. (Tel: (066) 39028 available through local markets and in Cork and Temple Bar)

● **Jam** James Mulchrone's shop and café pulses with the energy created by people who love making good food and people who love eating it. (Henry Street, Kenmare, Tel: 064 41591)

● **Kenmare Farmer's Market** Don't miss the fascinating trawl of food lovers – as well as artisans from farther afield – who corral together to bring you the best that the vicinity has to offer in the monthly specialist market. (Wednesdays from 9.30am)

● **Kerry Farmhouse Cheese** Sheila Broderick's territorial-style cheese come in a variety of flavours, and are another of the well-kept secrets of Kerry that deserve your attention. (Listowel, Tel (068) 40245)

● **Killorglin Farmhouse Cheese** Wilma O'Connor makes some of the most convincing and flavourful cheeses you can buy in Ireland. Sweet when young, the Killorglin cheeses mature to gorgeous milky expansiveness. Hunt them down! (Killorglin, Tel: (066) 61402)

● **The Pantry** One of the key addresses in Kenmare, Hugo's shop has all you need for scrummy cooking with the best local ingredients, as well as all the necessary bits and bobs. (Henry Street, Kenmare, Tel: (064) 42233)

● **Seancara Wholefoods** Philip Wheeler sells all the paraphernalia and foods you need in this busy Tralee healthfood store. (5 Abbeycourt, Tralee, Tel: (066) 22644)

● **The Skelligs Chocolate Co** Okay, so it's at the end of the earth – or at the end of the Ring of Kerry – but your kids will thank you forever for a trip to this magical little chocolate factory. The chocolates are as fantastic as their amazing packaging. (The Glen, Tel: (066) 947 9119 skelligchocolates.com)

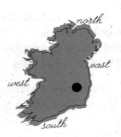

EATING OUT

● **The Ballymore Inn** The key Kildare address with the sharpest cooking: peerless ingredients are foremost in superb vegetable and pasta cooking, and the pizzas are just the best anywhere. Book well in advance or you won't get a table in the restaurant. Fine bar food also. (Ballymore Eustace, Tel: (045) 864585, Fax: 864747 Open: 12.30pm-3pm Mon, 12.30pm-3pm, 6pm-9pm Tue-Thur, 12.30pm-9pm Fri-Sat Lunch €€ & Dinner €€€)

SHOPPING

● **Harvest Kitchen**
Valerie and Susan offer a neat range of wines, the very fine Butlers Pantry takeaway suppers, and super sandwiches and coffee to eat in or take home. (1 Sallins Rd, Naas, Tel: (045) 881793, srouine@eircom.net)

● **Mary Morrin's Pies** You will find Mary's sensational pies at the Naas country market on Fridays, and they can also be bought at the house by arrangement. Pie heaven! (Kilcock, Tel: (01) 628 4411)

● **The Mill Wine Cellar** The Mill is an excellent wine shop with a very sharply composed selection of good bottles from all over the vinous world, and helpful service to back it all up. (Mill St, Maynooth, Tel: (01) 629 1022)

● **Vintage Crop** Audrey Walshe's shop mixes wine with flowers, so do pause to sniff the blooms as you ponder the evening's bottle. (Newbridge, Tel: (045) 440056)

County **Kilkenny**

KILKENNY CITY

● **Zuni** Zuni is funky and stylish, and seriously busy: if you can actually get a table here at the weekend, thank your lucky stars. The food is swish and modern, and well-crafted: roast vegetable and halloumi bruschetta; Ardsallagh goat's cheese tart with red onion marmalade; penne with pesto and roasted vegetables; spring roll with squashed cherry tomatoes and smashed olives (bit of a violent dish, that one). Great bar, and excellent rooms at very keen prices, so make a weekend of it. (26 Patrick St, Kilkenny, Tel: (056) 23999, Fax: 56400 info@zuni www.zuni.ie Open: 12.30pm-2.30pm, 6.30pm-10pm Tue-Sun, Dinner €€€€, Rates €€)

● **Shortis Wong** Chris Wong cooks some fab food-to-go in this excellent deli – cracking vegetarian spring rolls, lovely cheese wraps – really choice grub to graze on as you scour the shelves of this delectable emporium, packed with good things. Don't be afraid to ask Chris to make something according to your own specification! (74 John St, Kilkenny, Tel: (056) 61305)

● **The Gourmet Store** The toasted paninis are one of the main draws in the friendly Gourmet Store, witty and grand sanbos with witty and grand names, and there are loads of choice foods on sale also. (56 High St, Kilkenny, Tel: (056) 71727)

● **The Wine Centre** Edmund O'Keeffe's fine wine shop is as progressive as all the best Kilkenny businesses, and has recently created a wine storage solutions business to complement the excellent range of wines. (John Street, Kilkenny, Tel: (056) 22034)

KILKENNY COUNTY –

● **Calabash Bistro** This intimate little room, run by Jack and Brian, has thoughtful and carefully chosen dishes – courgette, potato and red onion galette with chive crème fraiche; twice-baked goat's cheese soufflé; vegetable calzone with tomato and herb fondue – and the puddings and wines are excellent. (Chapel Street, Bennettsbridge, Tel: (056) 27850)

● **Lavistown Cheese** Olivia Goodwillie's cheese is one of the glories of Irish cheesemaking, as distinctive and cerebral as the cheesemaker herself. It's a Caerphilly-style, sort of, pale white and crumbly, and if you can spare any, it is a particularly fine cooking cheese. Personally, it never gets near the stove in our house: the tense lacticity of the curd, with its slightly sharp lemony edge, means it needs nothing more than a glass of cool, light red wine. (Lavistown, Tel: (056) 65145, courses@lavistown.ie, lavistown.ie)

● **The Little Irish Apple Co** Look out for the scarce and very fine apple juices from this little company. (Piltown, Co Kilkenny)

● **Mileeven** Eilis Gough's range of jams, preserves, cakes, honeys and cakes are superbly made, the result of a questing and restless producer who never takes anything for granted. Just seek out that organic raspberry jam, for instance, and taste a superbly balanced, beautifully expressed jam, as good as you can buy. But, truthfully, it's invidious to single out only one product; all the Mileeven foods are superb. (Owning Hill, Piltown, Tel: (051) 643368)

● **The River Café** The Café has a good reputation for some imaginative salads in the Mediterranean style. (Bennettsbridge, Tel: (056) 27879)

● **The Water Garden** This atmospheric little room is run by the Camphill Community, and is great for real home-cooked, tasty food. (Ladywell St, Thomastown, Tel: (056) 24690)

● **Abbey Blue Brie** Don't miss the rich Abbey Blue Brie and the organic St Canice's sheep's milk cheeses (Cuffsborough, Ballacolla, Tel: (0502) 58559)

● **Anapamu** Global influences are the USP of this popular little restaurant in the centre of Portlaoise. (67 Main St, Portlaoise, Tel: (0502) 62200, Open Dinner €€€)

● **The Fruit and Nut Place** A smashing wholefood shop which is one of the very best you will find, and a great source of organically grown vegetables in particular. (1 Lyster Square, Portlaoise, Tel: (0502) 22239)

● **Gee's Jams** You will find Helen Gee's superb jams in good shops, so snap them up for a blast of pure fruit. (Abbeyleix, Tel: (0502) 31058)

● **Kingfisher Restaurant** Googi's Indian restaurant is in an old bank, and the good cooking has created one of the great success stories of the town. (Main Street, Old AIB Bank, Portlaoise, Tel: (0502) 62500, Open Dinner €€€)

● **The Kitchen** Jim Tynan's brilliant shop and restaurant are unmatched in the Midlands for sheer creativity and admirable hard work by the boss and his dedicated team. Superb. (Hynds Sq, Portlaoise, Tel: (0502) 62061)

● **Preston House** Allison Dowling's famous restaurant with rooms is at the southern end of Abbeyleix, and is every traveller's dream destination. (Main St, Abbeyleix, Tel: (0502) 31432, Fax: 31432, Open Lunch €€, & Dinner €€€, Rates €€)

● **Eden Plants** Rod Alston is a pioneer grower and plantsman, and every food lover should try this man's superlative produce, and source his plants for the garden. Herbs can be posted through the mail, so don't delay! (Rossinver, Tel: (072) 54122)

● **The Organic Centre** Archetypal educational centre with many brilliant short courses on all manner of organics and an inspirational space for growers and gardeners. (Rossinver, Tel: (072) 54338, theorganiccentre.ie)

● **Cheese Etc** Trevor Irvine's shop has all the artisan cheeses and many other brilliant foods. Cheese Etc is an essential address for food lovers. (Bridge St, Carrick-on-Shannon, Tel: (078) 22121)

EATING

● **Green Onion** The GO is a funky, tall room with fantastic music and, despite some occasional lapses, the cooking is tasty and moreish: smoked gubbeen and spinach tartlet; good felafels with tzatziki. (The Old Town Hall Building, Rutland St, Limerick, Tel: (061) 400710, Open daily, Lunch €€ & Dinner €€€)

● **Wild Onion** Scrummy American-style desserts are the big attraction in the WO – carrot cake; chocolate-walnut brownie; Southport slices; giant cookies – but their veggie burgers and Mediterranean vegetable sandwiches are also very good. (High St, Cornmarket, Limerick, Tel: (061) 44055, wildonioncafe.com, Open daily, Lunch €)

SHOPPING

● **Fine Wines** This is a small chain of wine shops with a good range of wines and beers. (Roches Street, Limerick, Tel: (061) 416501)

● **Greenacres** Marie Murphy also mans a stall at the excellent Saturday Limerick market in the Milk Market – a key event for food lovers – and for the rest of the week she has lovely food to eat or to go in the shop. (Cornmarket, Limerick, Tel: (061) 400334)

● Oisin Farmhouse Cheese

Rochus and Rose's cheeses are amongst the finest artisan cheeses made in Ireland, and their mature, hard goat's milk cheese should be labelled: "Warning: Deeply Addictive!". You will find the cheeses for sale in wholefood and specialist shops and markets, and don't miss them, for they are cheesemaking raised to the highest art form. Sublime. (Kilmallock, Tel: (063) 91528)

● The Oriental Food Store
The Oriental on Roches Street and the cavernous Cheong Heng Hong Chinese shop on Henry Street are key addresses for Asian speciality foods, and in particular for specialist vegetables in excellent condition. (Roches Street, Limerick, Tel: (061) 417139

● Terry's Speciality Wine Shop
Terry McCann's friendly wine shop is the best place in the city to hunt down choice specialist bottles of wine. (Denmark Street, Limerick, Tel: (061) 412445)

County
Longford

north
east
west
south

● Torc Café
Ruth McGarry-Quinn's lovely cafe and shop is a great place for tasty simple lunches of funky sandwiches, organic pastas, and some of the best sweet baking in Ireland. With great service from a dedicated team, you simply mustn't miss those fine Noodle House pastas, in particular. The Torc truffles, of course, are amongst the most scrummy and perfectly made chocolates and bonbons you will find anywhere in Ireland.(Ballymahon St, Longford, Tel: (043) 48277, Open daily, Lunch €)

● **The Aubergine Gallery Café** Steve Devlin's up-the-stairs restaurant in the centre of town is where food lovers head to for some real, true-flavoured modern cooking. It's a lovely room, with good service from young local folk who enjoy their work, and the food has lots of style. (1 Ballymahon St, Longford, Tel: (043) 48633, Open Dinner €€)

County **Louth**

EATING

● **No. 32 Restaurant** Susan Heraghty has always been an excellent vegetarian chef, and has a devoted following in 32. (Market St, Dundalk, Tel: (042) 933 1113, Open Lunch €€ & Dinner €€€)

● **Café Metz** A popular Dundalk destination. (Francis St, Dundalk, Tel: (042) 933 9106, Open Lunch, €€ & Dinner €€€)

● **Keyside Café Bar** A funky, popular room with a small selection of vegetarian dishes on a very global menu. (The Mall, Drogheda, Tel: (041) 984 4878, Open Lunch €€ & Dinner €€€)

SHOPPING

● **Bellingham Blue** Excellent raw milk blue cheese made by Peter Thomas from the family herd of Friesians. (Mansfieldstown, Castlebellingham, Tel: (042) 9372343 glydefarm@eircom.net)

● **Cooley Distillery** Look out for these fine whiskeys. (Riverstown, Dundalk, Tel: (042) 937 6102)

CARLINGFORD

. . . .

● **Beaufort House** A very professional and very comfortable B&B which makes for a great base for weekenders enjoying pretty Carlingford. (Ghan Rd, Tel: (042) 937 3879, Fax: 937 3878, mcaine@beauforthouse.net, Rates €€)

● **Georgina's Bakehouse** Lovely sweet baking and maternal, friendly service makes Georgina's a key player in Carlingford's lively culinary culture. (Tel: (042) 937 3346, Open daily, Lunch €)

● **Ghan House** Paul Carroll has powerhoused Ghan House into one of the most successful restaurants with rooms, beloved of weekenders from both Belfast and Dublin. Lovely cooking, great wines, a chill-out centre par excellence. (Carlingford, Tel: (042) 937 3682 Fax: 937 3772 ghanhouse@eircom.net www.ghanhouse.com Open: 10 January-23rd December, Dinner €€€€€, Rates €€)

● **Kingfisher Bistro** Mark Woods' cooking in the d'Arcy McGee grain store has won many admirers for an imaginative and fun style of modern food. (Tel: (042) 937 3716, Open Dinner €€€)

● **The Oystercatcher** A selection of pasta dishes – spinach and ricotta tortellini, vegetarian carbonara – is the order of the day in the friendly Oystercatcher, and walkers should note the fine, good value rooms which are perfect if you have been hiking the Taín Way. (Market Sq, Tel: (042) 937 3922, Fax: 937 3987, bmckev@eircom.net. Open Dinner €€€, Rates €€)

GREAT CARLINGFORD PUBS

O'Hare's pub is also known as The Anchor bar, and visitors should not miss a drink in this hugely lively old pub. You should also head out to Whitestone, to Lily Finnegan's Pub, a local secret which is mighty craic.

County **Mayo**

STAYING

● **Rosturk Woods** A serene location on the road out to Achill and Louisa Stoney's dynamic demeanour makes Rosturk the best address in the area, and a superb base for explorations on the western seaboard. (Mulrany, Westport, Tel & Fax: (098) 36264 stoney@iol.ie www.rosturk-woods.com Open: March-November, Rooms €€)

SHOPPING

● **Westport Thursday Market** The town with multiple pharmacies (really!) also hosts an excellent street market on Thursday when the produce of local artisans is for sale in all its magnificence. (Town Hall, Westport, Thursday)

County **Meath**

● **Boltown House** This pretty, demure house has fine rooms and sublimely delicious food from Susan Wilson that is country cooking defined. (Kells, Tel: (046) 43605, Fax: 43036 boltown@eircom.net www.hidden-ireland.com/boltown Open Feb-Nov, Dinner €€€, Rates €€)

● **Baking House Breads** Claire Mooney's organic breads are amongst the best you can buy, utilising superb ingredients and intriguing styles to make irresistible staples. Look for them in good stores and at the Dublin Food Co-Op. (Harlockstown, Ashbourne, Co Meath, Tel: (01) 835 9010)

● **The Celtic Brewing Co.** Look out for the Finian's Red Ale and Gold when in good wine shops: they are crisp, refreshing brews, packed with hoppy flavour even though they are pasteurised. (Enfield, Tel: (0405) 41558)

● **The Ryan Vine** Good bottles, a wine club and monthly tastings are the signatures of this splendid wine shop. (22 Trimgate Street, Navan, Tel: (046) 78333)

● **Teehan's The Noble Rot** Another choice wine shop in bustling Navan. (Navan, Tel: (046) 73489)

County
Monaghan

● **Castle Leslie** Sammy Leslie's capacious castle has been in the news thanks to hosting Fab Macca's wedding, but the real tunefulness here comes from Noel McMeel's sublime cookery. For us, McMeel is one of the great young chefs, and he has brought a brio to the castle that has made this one of the hottest addresses around. As Fab Macca knows, the vegetarian cooking is ace. (Glaslough, Co Monaghan, Tel: (047) 88109, Fax: 88109, info@castleleslie.com, www.castleleslie.com, Open Dinner €€€, Rates €€€)

10 GREAT
ROMANTIC PLACES

1

ASSOLAS HOUSE
CO CORK

2

BALLYMALOE HOUSE
CO CORK

3

BOLTOWN HOUSE
CO MEATH

4

BROOK LODGE INN
CO WICKLOW

5

CASTLE LESLIE
CO MONAGHAN

6

GHAN HOUSE
CO LOUTH

7

HALO
DUBLIN

8

POPPADOM
DUBLIN

9

THE TEA ROOM
DUBLIN

10

ZUNI
CO KILKENNY

County
Offaly

SHOPPING

● **Glenisk Fruit Yogurts** The Cleary brothers make the best yogurts with organic milk that you can buy, and for goodness sake don't miss the little pots of rhubarb yogurt, which are sublime. (Killeigh, Tullamore, Tel: (0506) 44259)

County
Sligo

● **Bar Bazaar** Coffee and treats in Bar Bazaar is one of the Sligo secrets. (Market St, Tel: (071) 44749)

SHOPPING

● **Carraig Fhada Seaweed** Frank Melvin's peerless seaweeds, sold under his Carraig Fhada label, are now available throughout the country, but West Sligo is where all the hard work and harvesting is done. Don't think about cooking pulses without some kombu, and do explore the sensual delights of Frank's seaweed bath packs, which are pure bliss. (Rathlee, Tel: (096) 49042)

● **Cosgrove's** We love Cosgrove's, a gentlemanly grocer's shop, the like of which is increasingly rare in our franchised lives. Step in the door, step back in time, bask in blissful nostalgia abetted by excellent foods and service. (32 Market St, Sligo, Tel: (071) 42809)

● **The Gourmet Parlour** The girls in The Gourmet Parlour make splendid sweet and savoury treats. (Bridge St, Sligo, Tel: (071) 44671.

● **Kate's Kitchen** Don't miss the inspirational Kate's Kitchen, one of the best specialist shops in the West, for all manner of good things. (3 Castle St, Sligo, Tel/Fax: (071) 43022, kateskitchen@eircom.net)

● **Noodle House Pasta** Ingrid Basler's brilliant Noodle House organic pastas have been one of the most successful specialist foods in recent years and for many people they have become one of the vital kitchen staples. Beautifully made with organic ingredients, they are beloved by children who just can't get enough of this pure goodness. (Curry, Tel: (071) 85589)

● **Octavius** Octavius is a splendid wine shop, run with commendable expertise and modesty by Michael Gramsch, and it is a great destination for some rare wines, as well as directly imported German varietals. (Grattan St, Sligo, Tel: (071) 71730 octaviusfinewines@oceanfree.net)

● **Tir na nOg** Mary McDonnell's Tir na nOg is and always has been one of the very best wholefood shops, inspirationally run by Mary with ceaseless energy and commitment. Whatever is good finds its way here, and is minded by a great team who share Mary's obsession with the greatest artisan and organic foods. (Grattan St, Sligo, Tel: (071) 62752)

10 RESTAURANTS
WITH GREAT MUSIC

1

ALDEN'S
BELFAST

2

CAFÉ PARADISO
CORK

3

CAYENNE
BELFAST

4

THE GREEN ONION
LIMERICK

5

HALO
DUBLIN

6

JACQUES
CORK

7

THE MERMAID
LISCANNOR

8

THE MERMAID CAFÉ
DUBLIN

9

101 TALBOT
DUBLIN

10

TRIBECA
DUBLIN

Tipperary

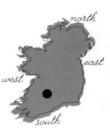

EATING

● **Angela's Restaurant** A buzzing centre-of-Clonmel room where Angela Ryan knocks 'em dead with lovely, feminine cooking, based around her trademark salads.
(14 Abbey St, Clonmel, Tel: (052) 26899, Open Lunch €)

● **Chez Hans** Hans has been a staple of the good life in Tipperary for over 30 years, but there is youthfulness in this kitchen, with fine cooking such as homemade tagliatelle with wild mushrooms, trademark risottos with char-grilled Mediterranean vegetables with cherryvine tomatoes; marinated Knockalara feta cheese with marinated cucumbers, and the desserts are sublime and irresistible. It's also a gorgeous room.(Cashel, Tel: (062) 61177, Open Dinner €€€€)

● **Clifford's at the Bell** Vegetarian choices are small in this cosy and intimate upstairs restaurant, but Michael Clifford's sublime skills makes sure they are not token, and pasta dishes such as penne with eggplant, pine nuts and a sharp fresh tomato and basil sauce with Parmesan are delivered with grace. (Cahir, Tel: (052) 43232, Open Dinner, €€€)

● **O'Tuamas** A hugely successful day-time restaurant with some of the finest desserts you can eat anywhere: if you renounced banoffi pie, just try the O'Tuama's version, and think again. Great, sharp cooking, and a room blessed with great energy. (Market Place, Clonmel, Tel: (052) 27170, Open Lunch €‑€€)

SHOPPING

● **The Apple Farm** Con Traas makes the best apple juice in Ireland, and he does so thanks to an application which is painstaking and passionate. Look out for the special cuvées of organic and selected juices, which show this magnificent grower's skill at optimum pitch. (Moorstown, Cahir, Tel: (052) 41459, signposted on N24 between Cahir and Clonmel)

● **Ballybrado** Josef Finke's excellent Ballybrado flours and biscuits are staples of every wholefood shop, and are of redoubtable quality. (Cahir, Tel: (052) 66206)

● **Baylough** Look out for these marvellous, and quite rare, cheeses, made by Anne Keating. One of Tipp's best-kept secrets, they are splendid cow's milk cheeses, and the smoked cheese is not to be missed. (Mount Anglesby, Clogheen, Tel: (052) 65275)

● **Cashel Blue & Crozier Blue** Cashel Blue is now a staple of every shop cheese counter, but don"t overlook its reliability and intrinsic quality. The new kid on the block is Crozier Blue, made with sheep's milk, and it's a demon new cheese, quite one of the best things you can buy. (Beechmount, Fethard, Tel: (052) 31151)

● **Cooleeney Camembert** Restless invention has seen a steady stream of new cheeses arrive from Breda Maher's brilliant company, with the delicious

Maugham soft cheese complementing the original Cooleeney, whilst the Dunbarra range is also superbly well made. (Moyne, Thurles, Tel: (0504) 45112)

● **Country Choice** Peter Ward is an artist. His canvas is composed of the specialist foods he sells in his glorious shop, his method is the most acute sympathy and understanding of those foods, crossed with a passionate desire to convince everyone of their goodness. Country Choice is unparalleled, shop and service exhibited as art. (25 Kenyon St, Nenagh, Tel: (067) 32596, countrychoice.ie)

● **Gleeson's Tea Rooms** Don't miss a chance to take tea in this fabulous, unchanged and unchanging old tea rooms in the centre of Nenagh. (37/38 Mitchell St, Nenagh, Tel: (067) 31518, Open Lunch €)

● **Tipperary Organic Ice Cream** Paddy and Joyce O'Keeffe's fantastic ice creams are amongst the most impressive of the new generation of speciality foods, their provenance and sheer chutzpah utterly winning. Hunt these down in good freezers. (Carrigeen, Clonmel, Tel: (052) 81905)

GREAT TIPPERARY PUBS

Dwan's Brew Pub
A stylish, swish room just down from the square in Thurles which is home to one of the country's best micro-breweries. The cooking could be a little sharper, however. (Thurles, Tel: (0504) 26007)

Kennedy's Pub
Head in here to a sublime country pub for a pint of Guinness as it used to be before Diageo made the drink into an alcoholic popsicle which is a travesty of itself. (Puckane)

County
Waterford

EATING AND STAYING

● **An Carn** Deuglan and Siobhan have worked hard to make the rooms in An Carn as cosy as the lovely restaurant, making An Carn a great escape. (Ring, Dungarvan, Tel: (058) 46611, Fax: 46614, ancarn@eircom.net, www.ancarn.com, Open Dinner €€€ Rates €€)

● **Hanora's Cottage** Extraordinary breakfasts, homely cooking, fantastic hospitality, a walker's paradise up in the mountains. (Nire Valley, Tel: (052) 36134. Open 6.30-9pm, Dinner €€€€, Room €€)

● **Powersfield House** A dynamic country house with truly great cooking, but do give Eunice some notice so she can augment the short dinner menu. (Ballinamuck West, Dungarvan, Tel: (058) 45594, Fax: 45550 www.powersfield.com Open: 7pm-10pm Thu-Sat, Dinner €€€€, Rooms €€)

● **Richmond House** Paul and Claire Deevy's house is one of the very best country house destinations, and the creativity shown in their vegetarian dinner menus is terrific: organic salad with Japanese cucumber and coriander dressing; fresh fettuccine with tomatoes, garlic and cream; tomato tartlet with local goat's cheese and pesto. Richmond is a peach of a place. (Cappoquin, Tel: (058) 54278, Fax: 54988 info@richmondhouse.net www.richmondhouse.net Open Dinner Mon-Sun (closed Sun off season), Dinner €€€€, Rooms €€)

EATING

● **The Tannery Restaurant** Paul Flynn doesn't offer a large choice of vegetarian dishes, but what he does offer shows the work of one of the most authoritatively creative cooks in Ireland. Even simple things such as quesadilla of goat's cheese with honey and marjoram shows the sort of inspired matching of unlikely herbs and other flavours that make his work so unique. Parmesan fritters with tomato and avocado salsa, or plum tomato and olive tart with feta are just as inspired and packed with flavour. Beautiful room, and great value for money. (10 Quay St, Dungarvan, Tel: (058) 45420, Fax: 45518 tannery@cablesurf.com www.tannery.ie Open: Lunch Tue-Fri & Sun, Dinner Tue-Sat, Dinner €€€€)

● **White Horses** This lovely, simple seaside room is renowned for some of the best sweet baking you can find, but Christine and Geraldine have a sure hand with the savoury things too: golden fried Brie with Julie's tomato chutney; Mediterranean vegetable and noodles with toasted sesame seeds; spinach and mushroom crêpe a la crème; tagliatelle with toasted Parmesan. A lovely friendly room with great service. (Main Street, Ardmore, Tel: (024) 94040 Open: 11am-11pm Tue-Sun (winter opening 11am-11pm Fri & Sat, 11am-6pm Sun) Closed January, Lunch €€, Dinner €€€)

● **The Wine Vault** David Dennison's restaurant is as well known for its excellent basement wine cellar as for the cosy, clubby restaurant itself. The mix of wines and bistro-style foods is always delightful. (High Street, Waterford, Tel: (051) 853444, fax: 853777, bacchus@eircom.net)

SHOPPING

● **Barron's Bakery** Craft bakeries in
Ireland are nowadays as rare as hen's
teeth, so thank heavens for the
continued existence of Joe and Esther
Barron's beautiful old bakery, where
the bread is still shaped by hand and
baked in huge old stone ovens. (Cappoquin, Tel: (058)
54045)

● **Crinnaghtaun Apple Juice** Julia Keane's
elegant and thirst-quenching juice is one of the great
West Waterford foods. Intensely flavoured, yet
beautifully balanced, it is a juice that can be drunk
with any food, and it's a pure definition of goodness.
Crinnaghtaun is widely available in shops and
supermarkets throughout the country.
(Cappoquin, Tel: (056) 54258)

● **Gallwey's Chocolates** Grichi
Gallwey's chocolates are quite unlike
any others, with brooding, lingering
flavours that have a mighty aftertaste.
The whiskey truffles and the coffee
truffles are intense, and superbly well
made. The newer pralines are just as
expert and seductive as the rest of the Gallwey range.
(Rockfield House, Tramore, Tel: (051) 381208)

● **Knockalara Cheese** A crumbly,
pale sheep's milk cheese is the
knockalara signature, but do look out
also for their very delicious feta
preserved in oil. (Cappoquin, Tel: (024)
96326)

● **Knockanore Farmhouse Cheese** Eamonn
Lonergan flavours some of his cheeses with herbs,
but the mature plain Knockanore is our favourite from
his range. (Ballyneety, Knockanore, Tel: (024) 97275)

County
Westmeath

north

east

west

south

EATING

● **The Left Bank Bistro** Located in Fry Place (ho, ho) Annie and Mary's cracking bistro is one of the great Midlands addresses with lovely, smart cooking: tortilla filled with creamy vegetables; goat's cheese with shaved fennel; excellent Left Bank house salads; good vegetable spring rolls. The atmosphere and service in TLB are exemplary. (Fry Place, Athlone, Tel: (0902) 94446, Fax: 94598 mail@leftbankbistro.com www.leftbankbistro.com Open 10.30am Tue-Sat, lunch noon-5pm, dinner from 6pm, Lunch €€, Dinner €€€€)

funky

STAYING

● **Temple Country House** Declan and Bernadette Fagan's petite and pretty country house offers some of the most imaginative vegetarian cooking you will find, as well as one of the great chill-out centres in the country. The spa treatments complete a picture of complete bliss, and it's only a few hours from the capital! Mrs Fagan creatively and knowledgeably caters for all special dietary needs, making Temple some sort of heaven. (Horseleap, Moate, Tel: (0506) 35118, Fax: 35008 info@templespa.ie www.templespa.ie Open: All year, except Christmas, Inclusive Rates €€€)

chic

THE BRIDGESTONE VEGETARIAN GUIDE **97**

● **Wineport Lodge** Ray and Jane's ambitious new wine hotel (the rooms are named after various shippers, importers and wine producers) offer superb rooms, though we hope they will shield the balconies off, one from the other, so one can enjoy breakfast looking out over the lake without being conscious of your neighbours. The cooking could do with a little sharpening up, but this is yet another great institution, and one of the great chill-out destinations. (Glasson, Tel: (0902) 85466, Fax: 85471, www.wineport.ie, www.lodge@wineport.ie, Open Lunch €, & Dinner €€)

DRINKING

● **Wines Direct** Paddy Keogh's wine firm is one of the very best in Ireland. Opinionated, well-informed, armed with dozens of good bottles sourced with unflagging energy by the man himself, this company delivers the lot: great wines, great service through the mails, great value, the true culture of enjoying wine. (Irishtown, Mullingar, Tel: 1800-579579, wines-direct.com sales@wines-direct.com)

● **Al Vinos** A splendid Athlone wine shop, with loads of great wines and fine foods. (Irishtown, Tel: (0902) 74589 alvinos@indigo.ie)

● **Cana** Cana is the wine destination in Mullingar, especially for rare Italian wines, and do turn up on Saturday mornings for the tastings. (10 Castle Street, Mullingar, Tel: (044) 42742)

SHOPPING

● **Corbetstown Goats Cheese** Anne Holton's excellent handmade goat's cheese is the speciality food to hunt down in the region. It's one of the most impressive of the new generation of farmhouse cheeses. (Corbetstown, Killucan, Tel: (044) 74845)

10 GREAT
SIGNATURE DISHES

1

MALAYSIAN LAKSA, STIR-FRIED BAK CHOI AND SHIITAKE
CHERRY TREE, CO CLARE

2

BUTTERBEAN CASSEROLE WITH CIDER
LENNON'S CAFE BAR, CARLOW

3

WATERCRESS RISOTTO, CANNELLONI BEANS STEW
CAFE PARADISO, CORK

4

ARTICHOKE POTATO CAKE, LENTIL VINAIGRETTE
JACOBS ON THE MALL, CORK

5

KNOCKALARA SHEEPS' CHEESE PROVENÇALE BEAN STEW
BALLYMALOE HOUSE, CORK

6

LEEK & MUSHROOM STROGANOFF, SAGE & GINGER
THE MILL, CODONEGAL

7

SQUASH & PARMESAN SOUP WITH CELERIAC
HALO, DUBLIN

8

CRISPY RICE & LENTIL CREPES WITH SPICED POTATO
SONAR GAON, DUBLIN

9

PEA MOUSSELINE, FONDANT POTATO & LENTILLES DU PUY
SHEEN FALLS LODGE, CO KERRY

10

RED PEPPER & FETA CHEESE MOUSSE, GRILLED ARTICHOKES
ALDEN'S, BELFAST

EATING

● **La Marine** Eugene Callaghan is one of Ireland's greatest cooks, and La Marine is one of Ireland's greatest rooms. This chef makes everything seem new; tagliatelle with broccoli, rocket and gorgonzola cream; potato rosti with horseradish crème fraîche; vegetable polenta cake, sublime desserts and wines, great service. (Kelly's Resort Hotel, Rosslare, Tel: (053) 32114, Fax: 32222 kellyhot@iol.ie www.kellys.ie Open: 12.30pm-2.30pm, 6.30pm-9.30pm Mon-Sun. Closed Dec-end Feb, Lunch €€, Dinner €€€€)

SHOPPING

● **Farmer Direct** It doesn't look like much – okay, it looks like a Nissen hut at the side of the road – but this enterprising and visionary collective of local growers and artisans is a fab destination with loads of great things for sale. (New Ross, Tel: (051) 420816)

● **Greenacres** James and Paula O'Connor are ambitious and knowledgeable wine buffs, whose service extends from humble wines to stellar clarets at wallet-breaking prices. But Greenacres also has excellent specialist foods for sale, making it a key south-east address. (North Main Street, Wexford, Tel: (053) 22975, greenacres.ie)

● **Mine Gabhar** Luc and Anne van Kampen's little truckles of Mine Gabhar ('minnie gower') goat's cheese are amongst the most enjoyable cheeses you can buy anywhere. A melting, creamy, snow-white interior is the result of sensational cheesemaking, and is worthy of your very best bottle of wine. (Ballynadrishogue, Blackwater, Tel: (053) 27331)

● **Only Natural** An excellent wholefood shop, with a sister branch on Castle Street in Enniscorthy. (79 North Main Street, Wexford, Tel: (053) 23236)

● **Pettitt's** This exemplary chain of independent supermarkets is one of the jewels of the south east, with superb foods, and great, motivated staff. Their wine selection is particularly fine. (Main St, Gorey, Tel: (055) 21722, The Duffry, Enniscorthy, Tel: (054) 36202, St Aidan's Shopping Centre, Wexford, Tel: (053) 24055, Wexford Rd, Arklow, Tel: (0402) 39770, pettitts.ie)

● **Friday Country Market**
In the Bull Ring, Wexford (starting time 9am).

● **St.Killian & St Brendan Brie** Paddy Berridge's excellent cheeses are amongst the best known of the Irish farmhouse cheeses, and are deservedly popular and successful. Always pleasing, their delicate, floral lacticity is a delight. (Adamstown, Enniscorthy, Tel: (054) 40560)

● **Stable Diet** Cakes, bakes, chutneys and salads are all produced by Stable Diet, and all are extremely good. (Yoletown, Broadway, Tel: (053) 31287 stablediet@eircom.net)

STAYING

● **Kelly's Resort Hotel** Parent heaven. Chill-out capital of the South-east. Wine lover's paradise. Romantic getaway. Children's favourite. Whatever accolade you want to personally bestow on Kelly's legendary resort hotel, it is worthy of them all. Everyone is made to feel special, so don't miss it. (Rosslare, Tel: (053) 32114, Fax: 32222, kellyhot@iol.ie, www.kellys.ie, Rates €€€)

● **Salville House** Salville is one of the sweetest country houses, with Gordon Parker's cooking some of the best, most imaginative that you can find, based on superb understanding of vegetables and herbs. (Enniscorthy, Tel: (054) 35252, Fax 35252 info@salvillehouse.com www.salvillehouse.com Open: All year except Christmas, Rooms €€)

County **Wicklow**

● **Avoca** The original branch of the mighty Avoca is a place of pilgrimage for many southsiders, who head here rather than cooking lunch at home. Join the queue – there is always a queue – and agonise over which of the delights to choose. There are also many wonderful foods for sale in the hip shop. Speaking of queues: what do you call eight Barbies in a line? A Barbiequeue. Sorry. (Kilmacanogue, Tel: (01) 286 7466, Fax: 286 2376; Powerscourt House, Tel: (01) 204 6070 info@avoca.ie www.avoca.ie Open: 9.30am-5.30pm Mon-Sun, Lunch €€)

● **The Brook Lodge Inn & The Strawberry Tree Restaurant** The visionary Brook Lodge is a marvel, whether you are escaping from the city – an hour north – getting married – such a cute church – or just enjoying Evan Doyle's inspirational hotel and restaurant. Many folk come down for the monthly organic market and take a long, leisurely Sunday lunch, whilst in the Strawberry Tree Restaurant, chef Frederic Souty shows just what can be done with organic and wild ingredients: deep-fried brie with capsicum vinaigrette; tomato and fennel sorbet; stack of vegetables with pesto and Arborio rice; penne with avocado, goat's cheese and chilli; aubergine caviar with wild herbs; vegetable pappardelle. They can get a little stretched at times, but this is a magnificent, up-for-it! crew, and a mighty place. (Macreddin Village, Aughrim, Tel: (0402) 36444, Fax: 36580 brooklodge@macreddin.ie www.brooklodge.com Open: 7pm-9.30pm Mon-Sat, Sun lunch 1pm-7pm, Dinner €€€€, Rooms €€€)

WICKLOW MARKETS

• The Brook Lodge Inn Sunday Market (Macreddin Village, Tel: (0402) 36444, Fax: 36580, brooklodge.com)
• The Golden Ball at Kilternan (Saturday 11am)
• North Wicklow Country Market (Scout Den, Kilcoole, Saturday 11am)
• Roundwood Market (Roundwood, Sunday 3pm)

SHOPPING

● **Ashford Food & Wine**
Daragh O'Loughlin's wine shop is a relative newcomer, but the boss has lots of experience in the trade. (Ballynahinch Road, Ashford, Tel: (0404) 40033)

● **Grangecon Foodstore & Café** Jenny Craigie's traiteur in hard-to-find Grangecon is much respected by locals for true, creative cooking, so hunt it down. (Grangecon, Tel: (045) 403982)

● **Murtagh's** Denise Cray's shop is a real treat, so go ahead; treat yourself. (The Square, Enniskerry Village, Tel: (01) 276 0404)

● **Nature's Gold** Brod Kearon has run this beacon of good food and good health in Greystones since before it was either fashionable or profitable. (1 Killincarrig Rd, Greystones, Tel: (01) 287 6301)

● **The Stone Oven** A lovely bespoke bakery with breads baked in traditional German style. A great institution. (Kingshill, Arklow, Tel: (0402) 39418)

● **The Wicklow Wine Company** An excellent wine shop with brilliantly chosen bottles and fine foods. (Main Street, Wicklow, Tel: (0404) 66767)

ORGANICS & BIODYNAMICS

Ballinroan Bio-Dynamic Farm
For our money, Penny and Udo Lange are the finest vegetable producers in Ireland, living proof of the merits of bio-dynamic farming. Everything they grow and produce is peerless, utterly of itself, packed with true natural energy, truly food for life. Contact Penny and Udo to join their box-delivery system, otherwise find the food in the Dublin Co-Op, Terenure market, and at their farm shop on Thursdays. (Kiltegan, Tel: (0508) 73278, Fax: 73424)

Organic Life
Marc and Adrienne Michel are the funkiest practitioners of organics you can find, and their produce, sold in their farm shop as well as certain outlets under the Organic Life label, is brilliant. (Kilpedder, Tel (01) 281 0545)

NORTHERN IRELAND

Northern **Ireland**

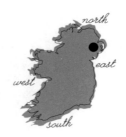

BELFAST

●●●●●●●●●●●

EATING

● **Alden's** Gorgeous food in a gorgeous room is the Alden's signature: steamed couscous with roasted vegetables and tomato sauce; mushroom curry with rice pilaff; beetroot risotto with goat's cheese and Parmesan; red pepper and feta cheese mousse with grilled artichokes. Great verve and imagination, fantastic service and wines. (229 Upper Newtownards Rd Belfast BT4 3JF Tel: (028) 9065 0079, Fax: 9065 0332 Open: Noon-2.30pm Mon-Fri, 6pm-10pm Mon-Sat (till 11pm Fri & Sat), Lunch €€€, Dinner €€€€)

● **Cayenne** Paul and Jeanne Rankin's signature restaurant has panache and punch in every way. The room is fabulously clandestine in style, the service is as poised and unpresumptuous as it has ever been, and Andy Rea's cooking is on the money: roast aubergine soup with coconut milk; borlotti bean risotto with courgette and rosemary butter is particularly terrific, goat's cheese puff pizza with roasted beetroot; lemon and fennel risotto with vodka; whilst there are always excellent salads, imaginative pastas such as spaghetti with artichokes and pea pesto and noodles and the best desserts: old clichés such as passionfruit tart with a kiwi salsa are achieved to perfection. The overall style is perhaps too unstructured for some, proving once again that the Rankins are ahead of contemporary tastes, but if you get the kick of Cayenne, it is indelible. (7 Ascot House, Shaftesbury Square, Belfast BT2, Tel: (028) 9033 1532, Fax: 90261575 reservations@cayennerestaurant.com www.cayennerestaurant.com Open: Noon-2.30pm Mon-Fri, 6pm-11.15pm Mon-Sat, Lunch €€, Dinner €€€)

● **Ginger** The toughest place to get a table in Belfast, but persevere for Simon McCance's cooking is fab and the room is thunderously alive and welcoming: one of the key city destinations you should not miss. (217 Ormeau Rd, Belfast BT7 3GG, Tel: (028) 9049 3143 Open: 5pm-9.30pm Tue-Sat, noon-3pm Sat, Lunch €, Dinner €€)

● **Nick's Warehouse** A Belfast institution at this stage, but the cooking is sharp as can be in Nick's and the room pulses with energy. (35-39 Hill Street, Belfast BT12 LB, Tel: (028) 9043 9690, nicks@warehouse.dnet.co.uk www.nickswarehouse.co.uk Open: Noon-3pm Mon-Fri, 6pm-9.30pm Tue-Sat, Lunch €€, Dinner €€€)

● **Porcelain** A gorgeous room, and Chris Buchanan is continuing the pioneering fusion cooking created by Niall McKenna in this super stylish boutique hotel. (Tensq 10 Donegall Square, Belfast BT1 5JD, Tel: (028) 9024 1001 Fax: 902 43210 mail@ten-sq.com www.ten-sq.com Open: All year, Dinner €€€€, Rooms €€€)

● **Café Renoir** This informal bakery and café can produce some delicious cooking, especially dishes such as their red curry, a beautiful amalgam of prime vegetables served searingly hot with perfect coconut steamed rice, and really good flourless chocolate cake. Care about the quality of ingredients used really shines through. (95 Botanic Avenue, Tel: (028) 9031 1300 Open all day Mon-Sat)

● **Shu** There aren't many vegetarian choices in the stylish Shu – salad of roast tomato with rocket, beetroot and Parmesan; pappardelle with cherry tomatoes, basil and pine nuts; goats' cheese and caramelised onion tart are the sort of Med–influenced ideas on offer – but the execution is deft, and the room itself is seriously cool and great fun. (253 Lisburn Rd, Belfast BT9 7EN, Tel: (028) 9038 1655, Fax: 9068 1632 eat@shu-restaurant.com www.shu-restaurant.com Open: 12.30pm-2.30pm Mon-Fri, 7pm-10pm Mon-Sat, Lunch €€, Dinner €€€)

● **Tavole** Johnnie Ritchie's restaurant really understands the ethos of Mediterranean cooking, so dishes such as three-tomato bruschetta with a bitter-sweet salad of frisée and basil oil, or white bean and fennel soup, are right on the money in terms of ingredients and execution. (479-481 Lisburn Road, Belfast BT9 7EZ Tel: (028) 9066 3211)

● **Zego** Aidan Rooney's petite coffee bar and bistro on Botanic Avenue offers well-regarded pasta dishes such as penne with tomatoes, parsley and capers and roasted peppers with feta, and indeed the flexibility of the menu means many vegetarian options can be easily assembled. (32 Botanic Avenue, Belfast, Tel: (028) 9080 8088, Open Lunch €, & Dinner €€)

EATING IN SHOPS

Equinox
At the rere of the immensely stylish Equinox shop on Howard Street there is a swish little café where the coffees are particularly good (and are served in Rosenthal china). Cooking can be erratic, ambience is always delightful.
(32 Howard St, Belfast BT1 Tel: 9023 0089, Open Lunch €)

Parks
Parks Café is a typically modern Belfast space, but the espresso is well made and their sweet things such as bakewell are good. Cool threads in the shop.
(Gt Victoria St, Belfast BT2, Tel: 9024 2394)

Smyth & Gibson's
Smyth & Gibson's Espresso Bar on Bedford Street has fine coffees, both to drink in or to go. Cool shirts out front. (Bedford House, Bedford St, Belfast BT2, Tel: 9023 0388, open daily)

Fulton's
Fulton's models itself on Dublin's Avoca Handweavers, mixing cakes and bakes with an emporium space designed to liberate your cash with minimum pain. (Boucher Crescent, Belfast Tel: 9038 2168, Open Lunch €)

SHOPPING

● **The Asia Supermarket** The success of Belfast's Chinese restaurants such as The Sun Kee and The Water Margin is based on the fantastic array of ethnic foods sold in the brilliant Asia Supermarket, easily the best Asian store in the country. Staff are extremely helpful, and if it isn't sold here, then it simply doesn't exist. (189 Ormeau Rd, Belfast, BT1, Tel: 9032 6396)

● **Café Paul Rankin** CPR in Fountain Street is a superb bakery and café, with beautiful breads and pastries and excellent day-time foods, which can be eaten in or taken away. The only problem can be getting a table 'round about lunchtime, when it gets mighty crowded. There is also a branch at Arthur Street, but Fountain Street is the destination of choice. (Fountain St, Tel: 9031 5090 Open daily)

● **Cargoes** Rhada and Mary's pioneering deli is one of the best places to both eat and shop in Belfast, and a vital address for food lovers on the Lisburn Road. Love and care are evident in every dish from the simplest sarnies through to the lunch specials, the work of two women who really respect the various cuisines which have influenced them. (613 Lisburn Rd, Belfast, BT9, Tel: 9066 5451)

● **Feasts** There is some excellent pasta cookery to be found in Feasts, on the Dublin Road, where Craig Nash runs one of the best shops and cafés in the city. Most folk don't understand pasta, but Nash and his crew make sublimely simple pasta dishes with impeccable ingredients that are fab. (39 Dublin Rd, Belfast, BT2, Tel: 9033 2787, Open Lunch €)

● **Olive Tree Company** Olivier Mandroualt's shop and café is tiny, but there isn't a carelessly chosen or carelessly cooked thing to be found in here, and dishes such as curried aubergine soup, or their excellent felafels in pitta with harissa sauce are beautifully delivered. NOTE: Change of ownership at time of going to press. (353 Ormeau Road, Belfast, BT1, Tel: 9064 8898 Olivier@olivetreeco.fsnet.co.uk)

● **Yellow Door Deli** Simon Dougan's pivotal deli is sister to the main branch in Portadown, and like that oasis of good food, the Lisburn Road branch is blessed with great, imaginative, creative cooking, and unmissable breads and pastries which – like everything else – are of benchmark standard. A couple of tables for al fresco lunches when the sun is shining complete the picture of a totally switched-on operation. (427 Lisburn Rd, Belfast, Tel: 9038 1961)

MARKET! MARKET! MARKET!

The Belfast Saturday Market, at the old St. George's Indoor Market across from the Waterfront Hall, is the best thing to have hit the city in yonks. There is such energy and excitement here on a Saturday morning that you will wind up spending far, far more money than you ever imagined, but don't let that stop you. Everything from Italian wine, to pomegranates, to the North's only artisan cheeses, to the best organic vegetables, organic eggs, and sparkling organic produce from Culdrum Farm are sold here by smartly-aproned and be-hatted stallholders. You seek cinnamon-flavoured apple juices? Step right up. Drumkeel cheese? It's here, all the way down from the far north coast. Aghadowey potatoes? Not a bother: fill up a big bag of these peerless potatoes. Sweet things from Piece of Cake (ho, ho)? They have them. Breads from Miller's bakery? Choose those soda farls, they are ace. You need vegetables and fruit from Philip McKee of Newtownards? The man is here himself to help you choose local vegetables in their prime, and imported specialities which are vital. What about Mount Sperrin ice cream? Dig deep in the freezer. Freshly picked organic beans? Grab a bag. There is no buzz in Belfast quite like the buzz of the Saturday Market. Don't miss it.

10 PLACES
FOR STYLE LOVERS

1

ALDENS
BELFAST

2

THE BROOK LODGE INN
MACREDDIN, CO WICKLOW

3

CAYENNE
BELFAST

4

CRAWFORD GALLERY CAFÉ
CORK

5

GINGER
BELFAST

6

HALO
DUBLIN

7

MERMAID CAFÉ
DUBLIN

8

NIMMOS
GALWAY

9

PORCELAIN
BELFAST

10

THE TEA ROOM
DUBLIN

ANTRIM

● **The Moat Inn** A splendiferous little country house, which is a style-lover's dream destination. Rachel Thompson's tasty cooking completes the bliss. (12 Donegore Hill, Templepatrick, Co Antrim, BT41 2HW Tel: (028) 9443 3659 Fax: 9443 3726 themoatinn@talk21.com Open: Open all year. Rates €€)

ARMAGH

● **Yellow Door Deli & Patisserie** Simon Dougan's brilliant deli and patisserie serves truly delicious breakfasts – French toast with maple syrup; blueberry pancakes; lovely ciabattas – and delectable lunches – Asian noodle soup; creamy lentil soup, served with a fantastic array of breads – as well as the most lip-smacking breads and traiteur foods you can find to take away. (74 Woodbridge St, Portadown, Tel: (028) 3835 3528 Open 9am-5pm)

DOWN

EATING

● **The Bay Tree** If you don't love Sue Farmer's cooking to bits, then you are seriously uncool, for this cook has a gifted touch that makes irresistible food. (118 High Street, Holywood, Tel: (028) 9042 1419 Open daily, Lunch €)

● **The Buck's Head Inn** Alison and Michael Carruther's pretty bar and restaurant has a high reputation in South Down for well-tuned cooking, and dishes such as terrine of aubergine, ricotta and roast red pepper are clever and accomplished. (77 Main St, Dundrum, BT33 OLU, Tel: (028) 4375 1868, Fax: 4375 1898, Open Lunch € & Dinner €€)

● **The Duke Restaurant** Currently the hottest spot in south Down, Ciaran Gallagher's upstairs restaurant is roaringly popular. Vegetarians are offered the chef's surprise, whatever ingredients inspire this creative cook on the day. (Warrenpoint, Tel: (028) 4175 2084, Open Dinner €€€)

● **Fontana** Colleen Bennett's upstairs restaurant is the Holywood hot spot, with great pastas and risottos and some deftly delivered ethnic dishes. (61a High Street, Holywood, Co Down, Tel: (028) 9080 9908, info@fontanarestaurant.com www.fontanarestaurant.com Open: noon-2.30pm Mon-Sat, 5pm-9.30pm Mon-Sat (from 6.30pm-10pm Sat), 11am-3pm Sun brunch, Lunch €€, Dinner €€€)

● **The Ganges** Terrible decor, but some excellent Indian cooking has made this Indian restaurant one of the staples of Holywood eating, with the many vegetarian choices in the takeaway menu very popular with locals. (47-49 High Street, Holywood, Tel: (028) 9042 1218, Lunch & Dinner €€)

SHOPPING

● **Camphill Organics** Camphill is a pioneering vegetarian cafe, bakery and wholefood shop, which also sells brilliant organic vegetables, lots of them sourced from John McCormick, a fabulous organic grower who also operates a box system within the region. Don't miss the hummus and pittabread, and enquire about the box delivery system in the shop. (Shore Rd, Holywood, Tel: (028) 9042 3203 Open Lunch €)

● **Sea Salt Delicatessen** Caroline Fitzpatrick's informal two-sittings per evening restaurant is the smash hit of Newcastle. Some don't like the rush involved in 2 sittings, but the craic is good. (Central Promenade, Newcastle, Tel: (028) 4372 5027)

● **Strangford Cottage** Elegant, stylish house which is a perfect base for exploring South Down. (Strangford Cottage, Strangford, Co Down, BT30 7NF, Tel: (028) 4488 1208, Fax: (028) 4488 1256, m.e.thornton@genie.co.uk Open: Mar-Sept. Off season by special arrangement., Rates €€)

NORTHERN WINE MERCHANTS

• James Nicholson and his team, of Crossgar, have won the award of regional wine merchant in the International Wine Challenge so often that you might reckon they would relax and take it easy. Not a bit of it: Jim and his team criss-cross the globe ceaselessly for fantastic new discoveries, and find them with a regularity which borders on the unbelievable: every time a newsletter comes through the door or is sent via their benchmark web site, there are brilliant new bottles. The shop is also a most gorgeous emporium: step in here and say goodbye to self-control! (Killyleagh St, Crossgar, Co Down, Tel: (028) 4483 0091, jnwine.com)

• Compendium Wine Merchants is a spiffing shop on Alanbrooke Road, just down from Ulster Weavers, where Neil Groom takes care of front-of-house, and the list and service are both of benchmark standards. Whilst Compendium remains less well known than other wine merchants, this situation won't remain so for long, for this is a dynamic wine company, with every bottle chosen with extreme care and informed expertise. A model merchant, moving fast. (Alanbrooke Rd, Belfast, Tel: (028) 9079 1197 www.compendiumwines.com)

• In Belfast, the McAlindon family's Direct Wine Shipments wears its years lightly and seems as youthful a business as ever, always extending its range with new discoveries (South Africa most recently), whilst remaining very strong indeed in the regions of Spain (a particular passion) and Italy. (Corporation Square, Belfast, Tel: (028) 9050 8000)

• The newest kid on the block for wine lovers to take note of is R&R Wines, run by Robert Neill. Mr Neill and his team are Australian specialists, and whilst this is a young company, there is passion for the vine aplenty here, so expect to hear a lot more about R&R in the future. (Ell's Fine Wines, Dobbin Road, Portadown Tel: (028) 3833 2306 Fax: 3833 6326)

MORE DRINK!

● **Barnhill Apple Juice** Made by Kenneth Redmond near Portadown, we like this served very cool, when the effervescent bouquet is shown at its best. Hunt the varieties down in the Belfast market.

● **Cumwin's Apple Juice** Cumwin's is hard to find, but it's a fine apple juice, pressed on the farm near Dungannon, delivered and sold locally.

● **Hilden Brewing Co** Hilden is the original craft brewer in Ireland, and Seamus Scullions brews are excellent, especially the Great Northern Porter (Hilden, Lisburn, Tel: (028) 2884 6663)

DERRY
● ● ● ● ● ● ● ●

● **Ditty's Bakery** Robert Ditty produces the very finest oatcakes you can buy, reason enough to make the journey to their shops in Magherafelt and Castledawson. Everything baked and cooked here is of superb quality, an inspiring craft business. (33 Rainey Street, Magherafelt, Tel: (028) 7963 3944; Castledawson, Tel: 0794 68243 dittybky@aol.com)

10 GREAT
WHOLEFOOD SHOPS

1
NATURE'S GOLD
WICKLOW

2
OPEN SESAME
ENNIS

3
ORGANIC OASIS
SCHULL

4
ORGANICO
BANTRY

5
SIMPLE SIMON
DONEGAL

6
THE PANTRY
KENMARE

7
QUAY CO-OP
CORK

8
TIR NA NOG
SLIGO

9
WELL & GOOD
MIDLETON

10
YIN YANG
SKIBBEREEN

INDEX

C

N

O

P

Q

R

Also from Estragon Press...

● In this provocative book, John McKenna offers a radical analysis of how restaurants operate, and why some restaurants succeed where others fail.

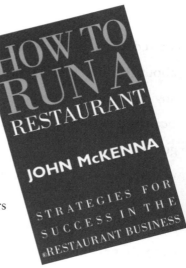

HOW TO RUN A RESTAURANT

JOHN McKENNA

STRATEGIES FOR SUCCESS IN THE RESTAURANT BUSINESS

● Examining the business from the position of a customer and a critic, McKenna analyses the factors which contribute to success, and explores the decisions that have to be understood by anyone who is either already running a restaurant, or considering opening a new restaurant.

● Practitioners and students will find the book an exhilarating intellectual exploration of one of the most mercurial and fascinating industries and entertainments in the world.

The Bridgestone Guides on the web

To access up-to-the-minute information about Ireland's food culture, and to discover any changes or alterations that may have occurred with the entries in the Bridgestone guides, visit:
www.bridgestoneguides.com

As well as a monthly newsletter, **megabytes,** bridgestoneguides.com brings you up-to-date information on the entries in the Bridgestone 100 Best Guides, as well as a host of news on Irish food.

Go on line for the good news...

VISIT:
www.bridgestoneguides.com

megabytes

is a fun, informative and up-to-the-minute e-zine written by John McKenna and a host of contributors, bringing you the vital news and views on the world of Irish and international food.

- **Restaurant reviews**

- **Seasonal recipes**

- **Readers' reports**

- **Campaigns to protect our food culture**

- **Competitions with great prizes**

- **Special offers**

- **A food lover's noticeboard**

visit **bridgestoneguides.com** and sign up! It's completely free!

For up-to-the-minute news on food matters in Northern Ireland, visit:

www.foodstuffireland.com

CAROLINE WORKMAN lets you have all the info on the hottest new places to eat out, the newest food lover's news and lots more besides.

Sign up & subscribe!

The Bridgestone food lover's guides to Ireland:

The Traveller's Guide

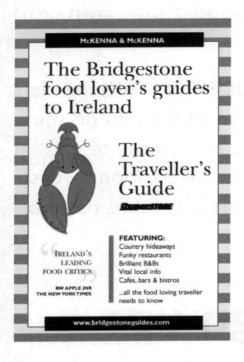

Here, in a single, compact volume is all the information the food lover needs to access the best places to eat and stay in Ireland. From the simplest pubs with real cooking, to the cutting edge of contemporary Irish cuisine, the Traveller's Guide will tell you the vital who, what and where throughout the highways and byways of Ireland.

The Bridgestone food lover's guides to Ireland:

The Shopper's Guide

With succinct wit and humour, the Shopper's Guide tells you who are the most important artisan producers in Ireland, and exactly where you can source and discover the fabulous foods they produce. If you want the inside track on Ireland's glorious food culture, you need to travel with the Shopper's Guide.

The Bridgestone 100 Best ...

'Contentious? Yes. Provocative? Absolutely. Supremely well written? Undoubtedly. John & Sally McKenna's 100 Best Restaurants and 100 Best Places to Stay prove once again to be the benchmark by which other guides are measured. In the quest for the best in the respective fields of accommodation and sustenance, the McKennas and their team have pulled out all the stops there are to pull out. The result is a smart, pocket and glove compartment-friendly pair of slim books with all the information you need for a sound sleep and a comfortably full stomach. Indispensable? That too.'

– Cara Magazine

• The Bridgestone 100 Best Restaurants in Ireland
• The Bridgestone 100 Best Places to Stay in Ireland

Published annually by Estragon Press since 1992